Success
Assessment Papers

Non-Verbal Reasoning

age 10 – 11

Pamela Macey

paper number for
quick reference

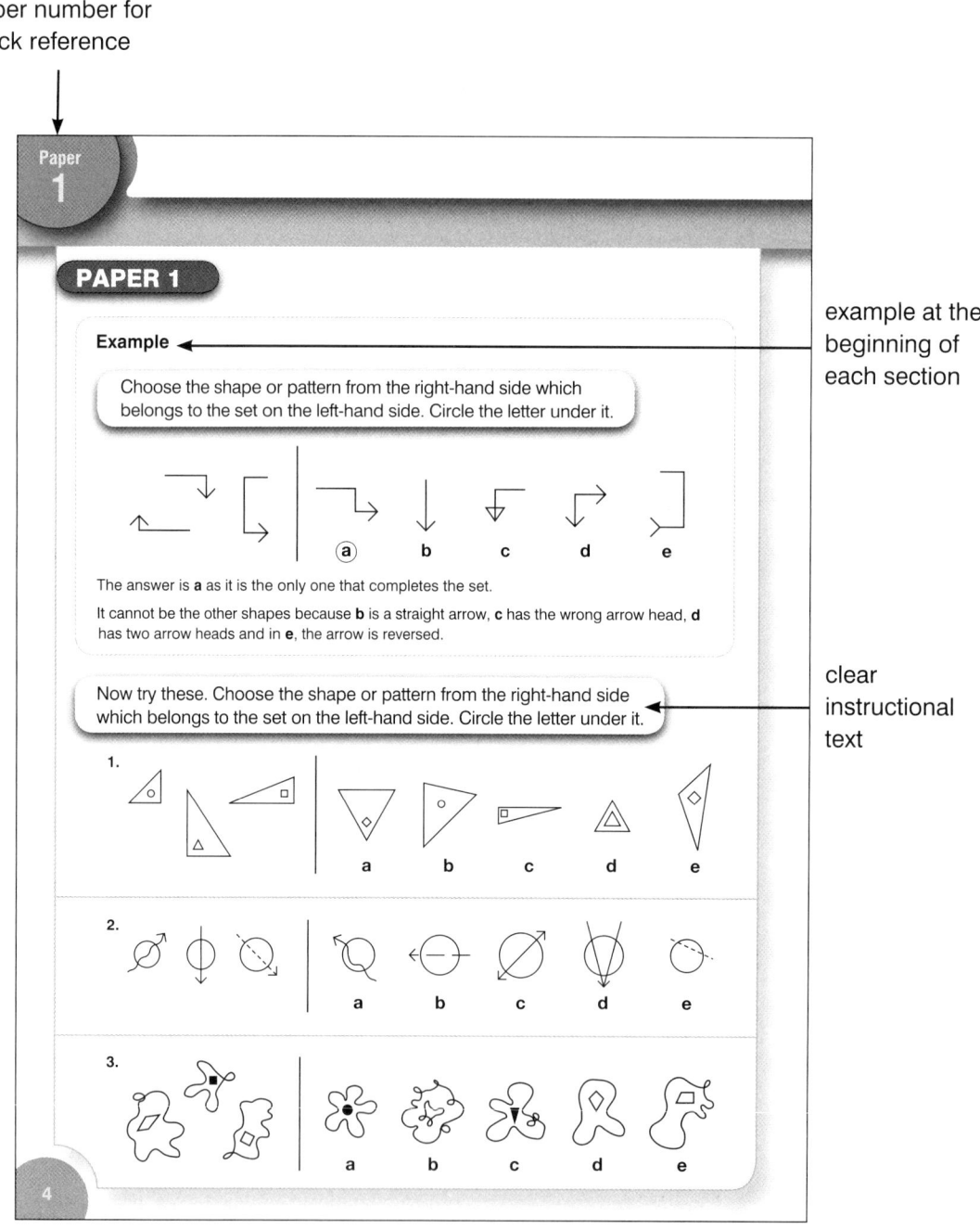

Paper
1

PAPER 1

example at the
beginning of
each section

Example

Choose the shape or pattern from the right-hand side which
belongs to the set on the left-hand side. Circle the letter under it.

a   b   c   d   e

The answer is **a** as it is the only one that completes the set.

It cannot be the other shapes because **b** is a straight arrow, **c** has the wrong arrow head, **d**
has two arrow heads and in **e**, the arrow is reversed.

Now try these. Choose the shape or pattern from the right-hand side
which belongs to the set on the left-hand side. Circle the letter under it.

clear
instructional
text

1.

a   b   c   d   e

2.

a   b   c   d   e

3.

a   b   c   d   e

4

Contents

PAPER 1

Example

Choose the shape or pattern from the right-hand side which belongs to the set on the left-hand side. Circle the letter under it.

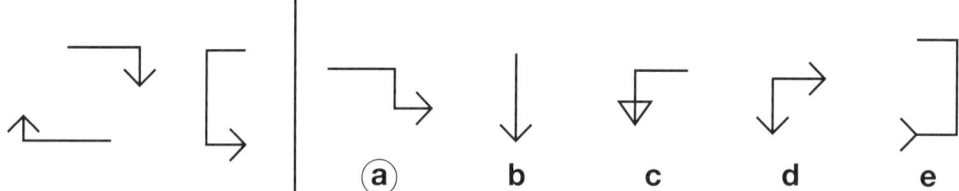

The answer is **a** as it is the only one that completes the set.

It cannot be the other shapes because **b** is a straight arrow, **c** has the wrong arrow head, **d** has two arrow heads and in **e**, the arrow is reversed.

Now try these. Choose the shape or pattern from the right-hand side which belongs to the set on the left-hand side. Circle the letter under it.

1.

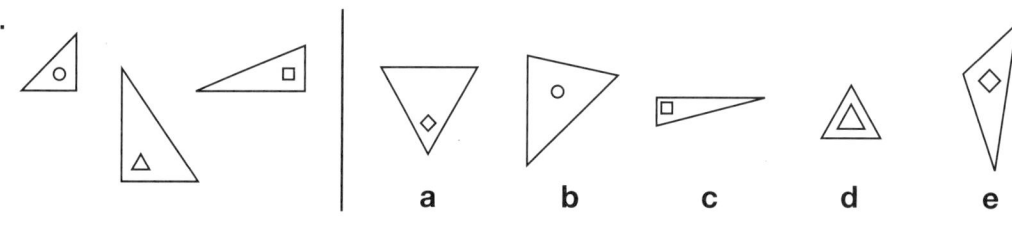

2.

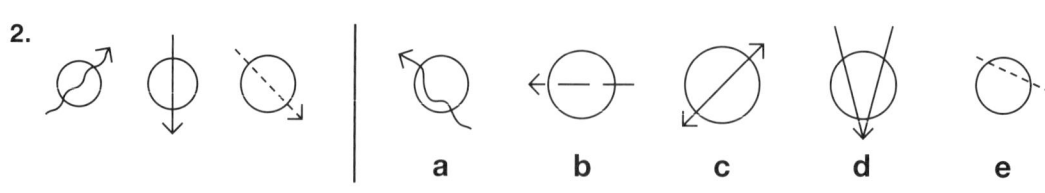

3.

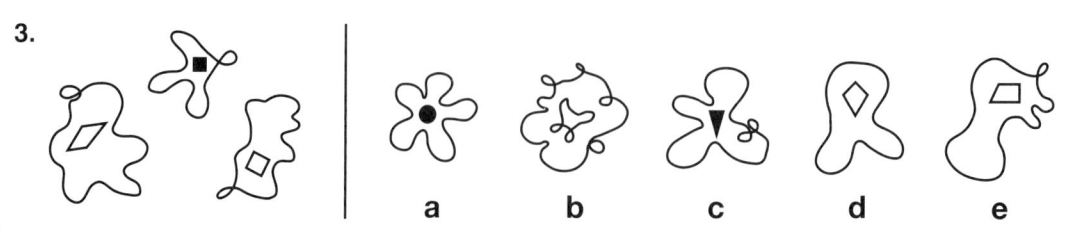

4.

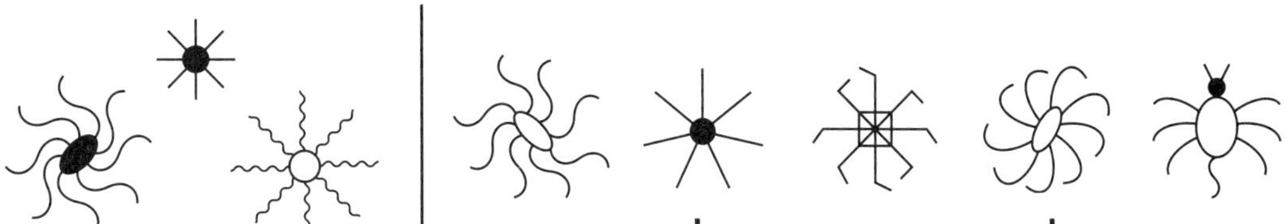

| a | b | c | d | e |

5.

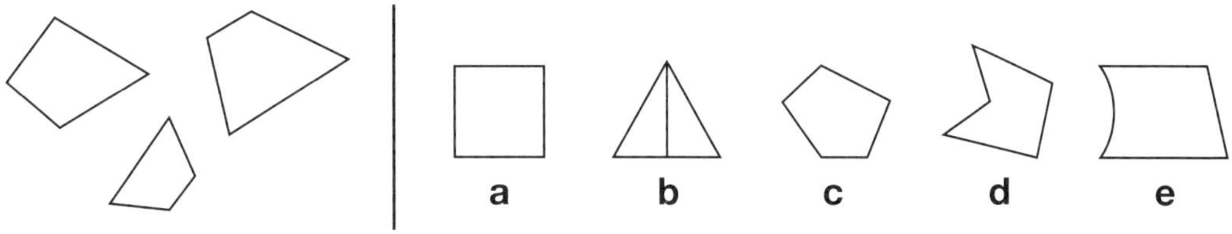

| a | b | c | d | e |

6.

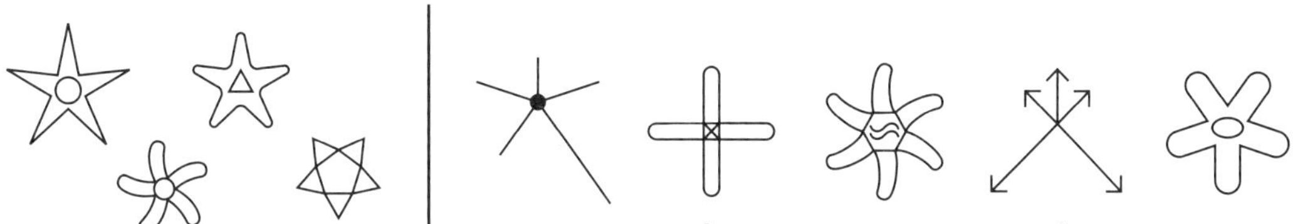

| a | b | c | d | e |

7.

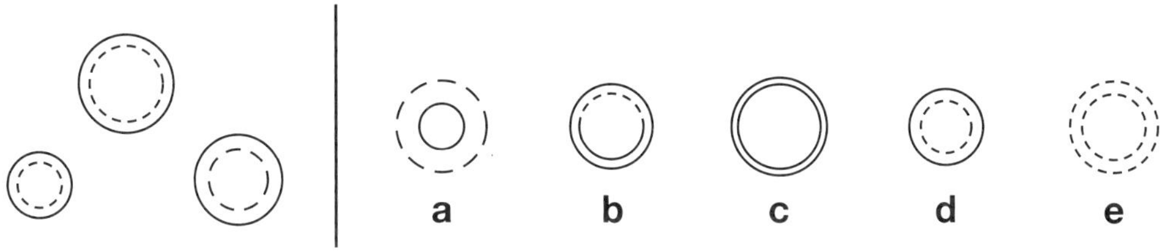

| a | b | c | d | e | /7

Example

Complete the grid by finding the missing square.
Circle the letter under the square.

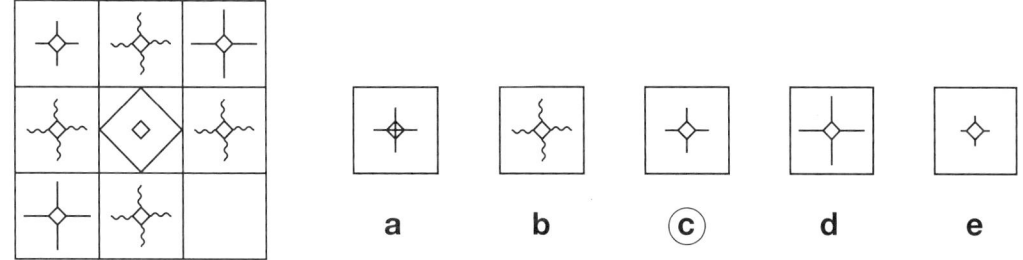

a   b   ⓒ   d   e

The answer is **c** because the outer squares of the grid are the same on the diagonal.

Now try these. Complete the grid by finding the missing square.
Circle the letter under the square.

8.

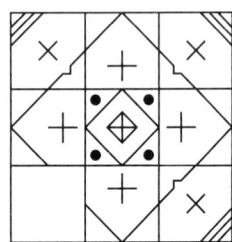

@	G	⊙	G	@
a	b	c	d	e

9.

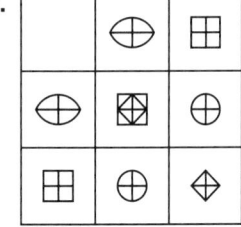

×	×	+	×	+
a	b	c	d	e

10.

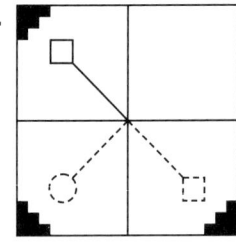

⊞	⊕	◈	◈	◈
a	b	c	d	e

11.

a	b	c	d	e

12.

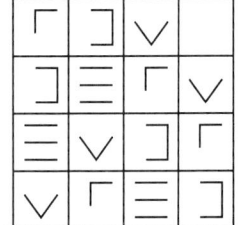

☰	∧	⊏	⌐	∨
a	b	c	d	e

13.

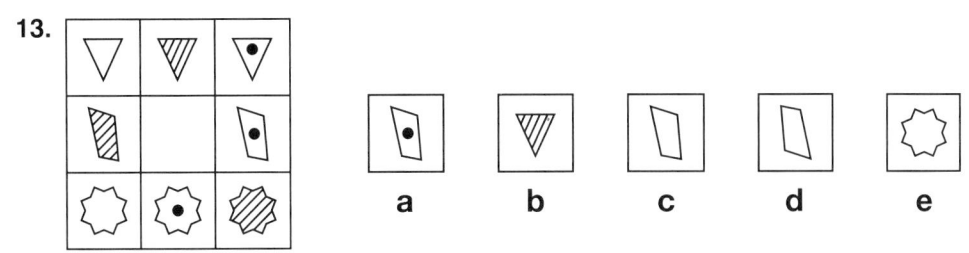

a   b   c   d   e

14.

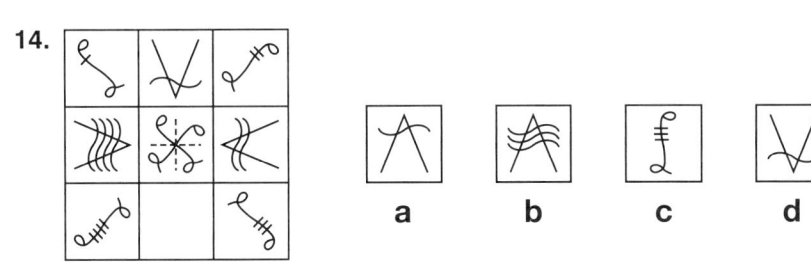

a   b   c   d   e

/7

Example

> Look at the patterns and letter codes to work out the new code. Circle the letter under the code.

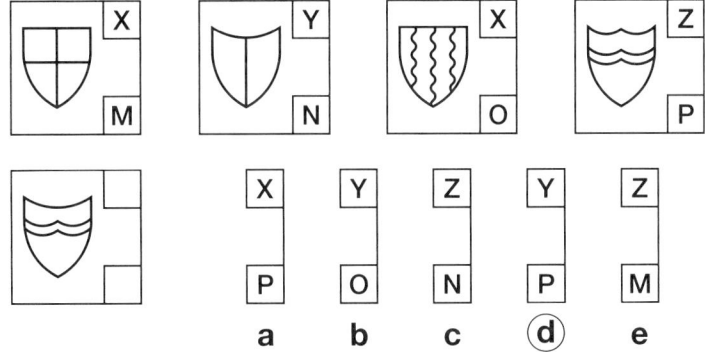

a   b   c   d   e

The answer is **d**. X, Y and Z are the codes for the shield shape. M, N, O and P are the codes for the patterns on the shields. In this case, the shield is Y and the pattern is P, so **d** is circled.

Now try these. Look at the patterns and letter codes to work out the new code. Circle the letter under the code.

15.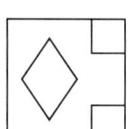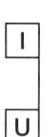

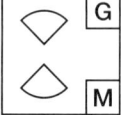

I	I	J	H	J
U	S	T	U	S
a	**b**	**c**	**d**	**e**

16.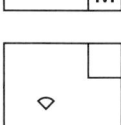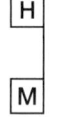

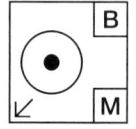

H	G	H	H	G
M	O	O	N	N
a	**b**	**c**	**d**	**e**

17.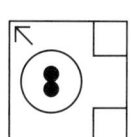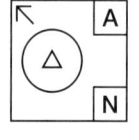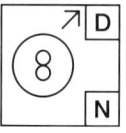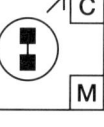

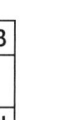

B	D	C	A	D
N	N	N	M	M
a	**b**	**c**	**d**	**e**

18.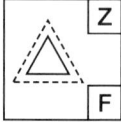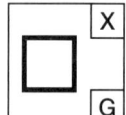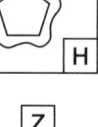

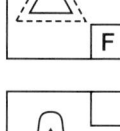

Z	Y	Z	W	X
H	F	G	H	F
a	**b**	**c**	**d**	**e**

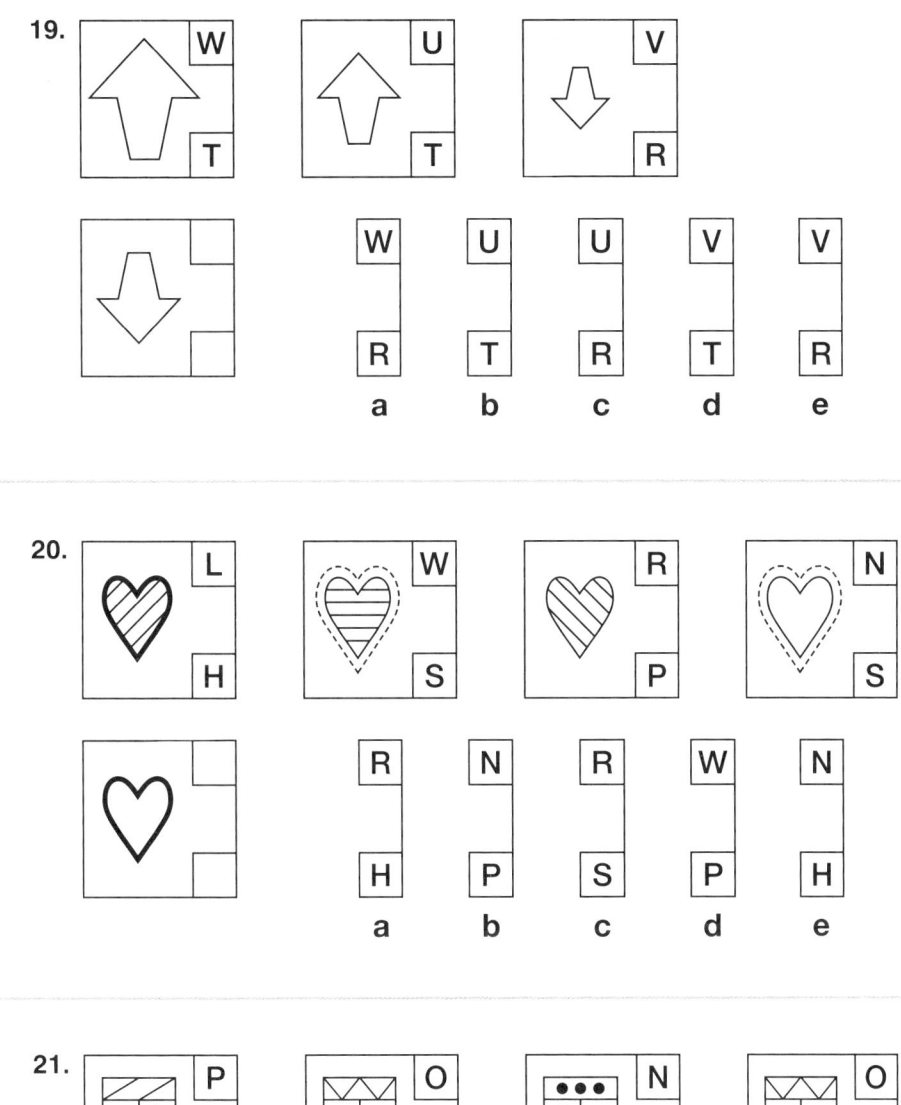

19.

20.

21.

/7

Example

Find the shape or pattern which completes the sequence. Circle the letter under it.

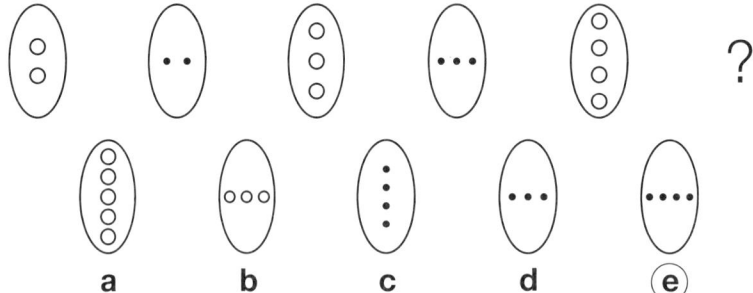

The answer is **e** because the pattern is large circles in a vertical line, followed by the same number of small black circles in a horizontal line.

Now try these. Find the shape or pattern which completes the sequence. Circle the letter under it.

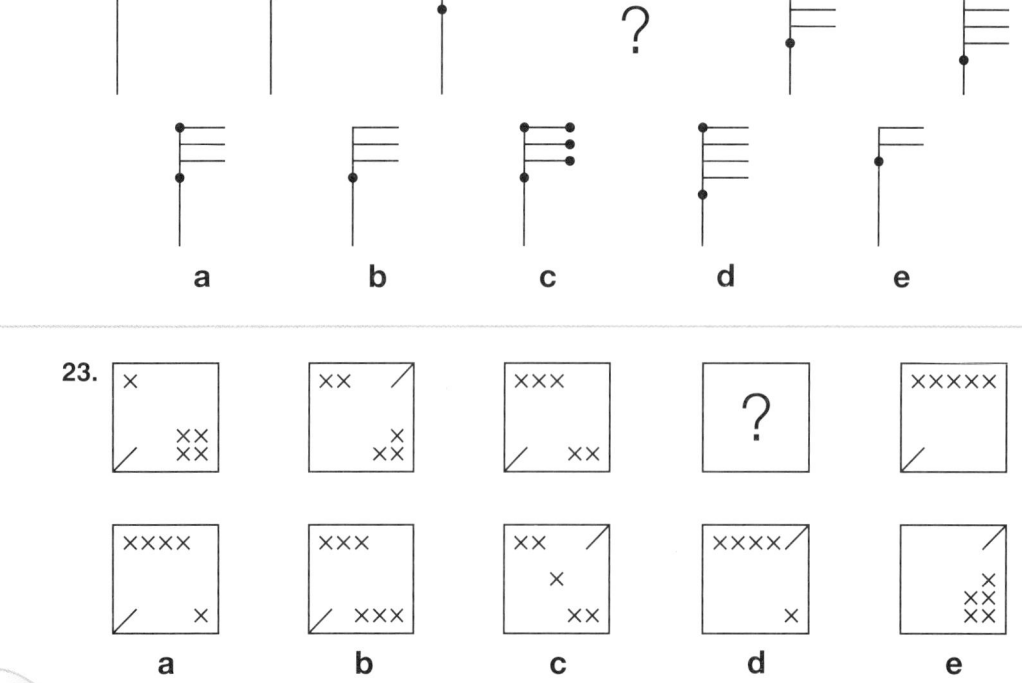

24.

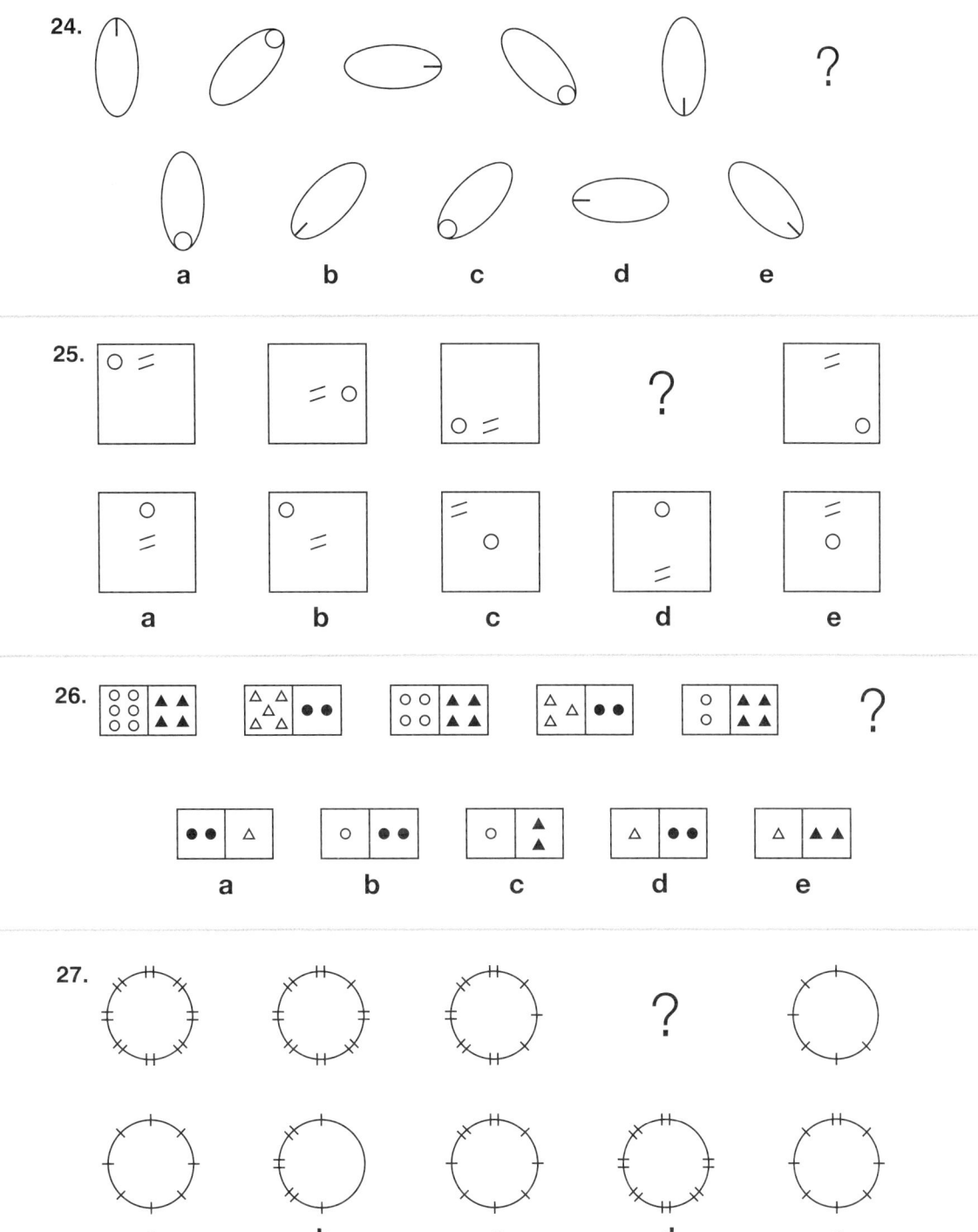

25.

26.

27.

28.

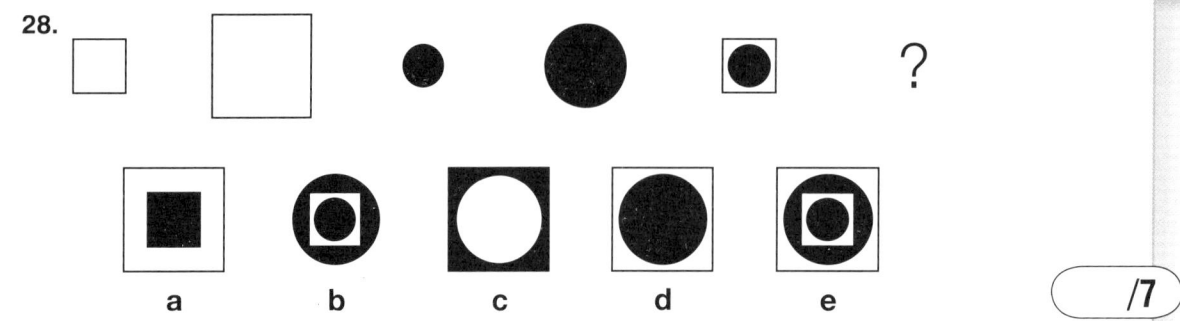

a   b   c   d   e

/7

Example

Match the missing part of the second pair in a similar way to the first pair. Circle the letter under the missing part.

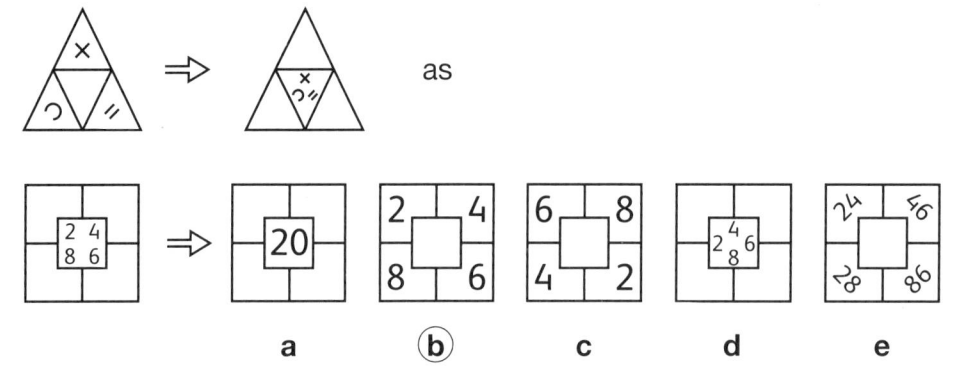

a   b   c   d   e

The answer is **b**.

Now try these. Match the missing part of the second pair in a similar way to the first pair. Circle the letter under the missing part.

29.

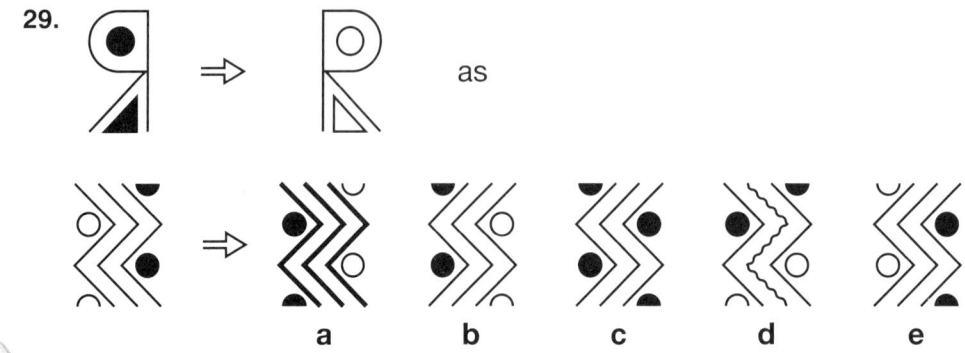

a   b   c   d   e

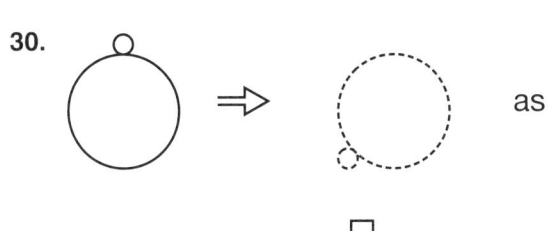

30.

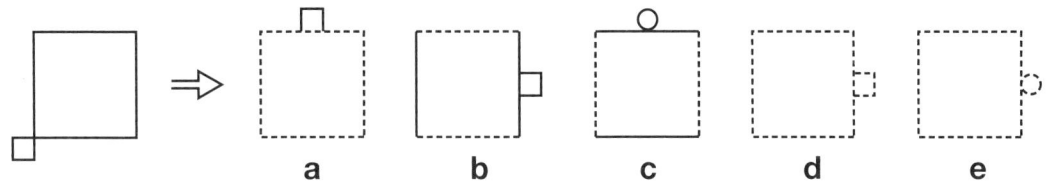

a   b   c   d   e

31.

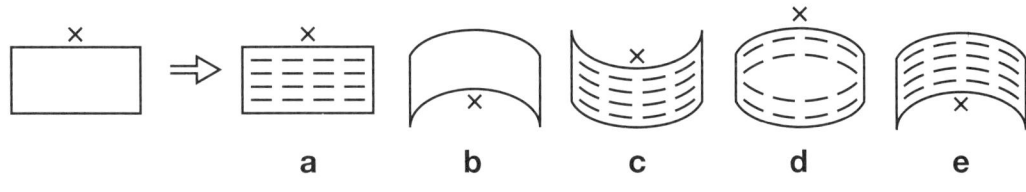

a   b   c   d   e

32.

a   b   c   d   e

33.

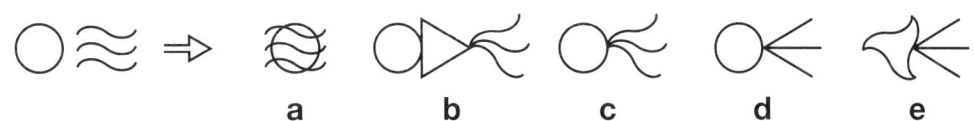

a   b   c   d   e

34.

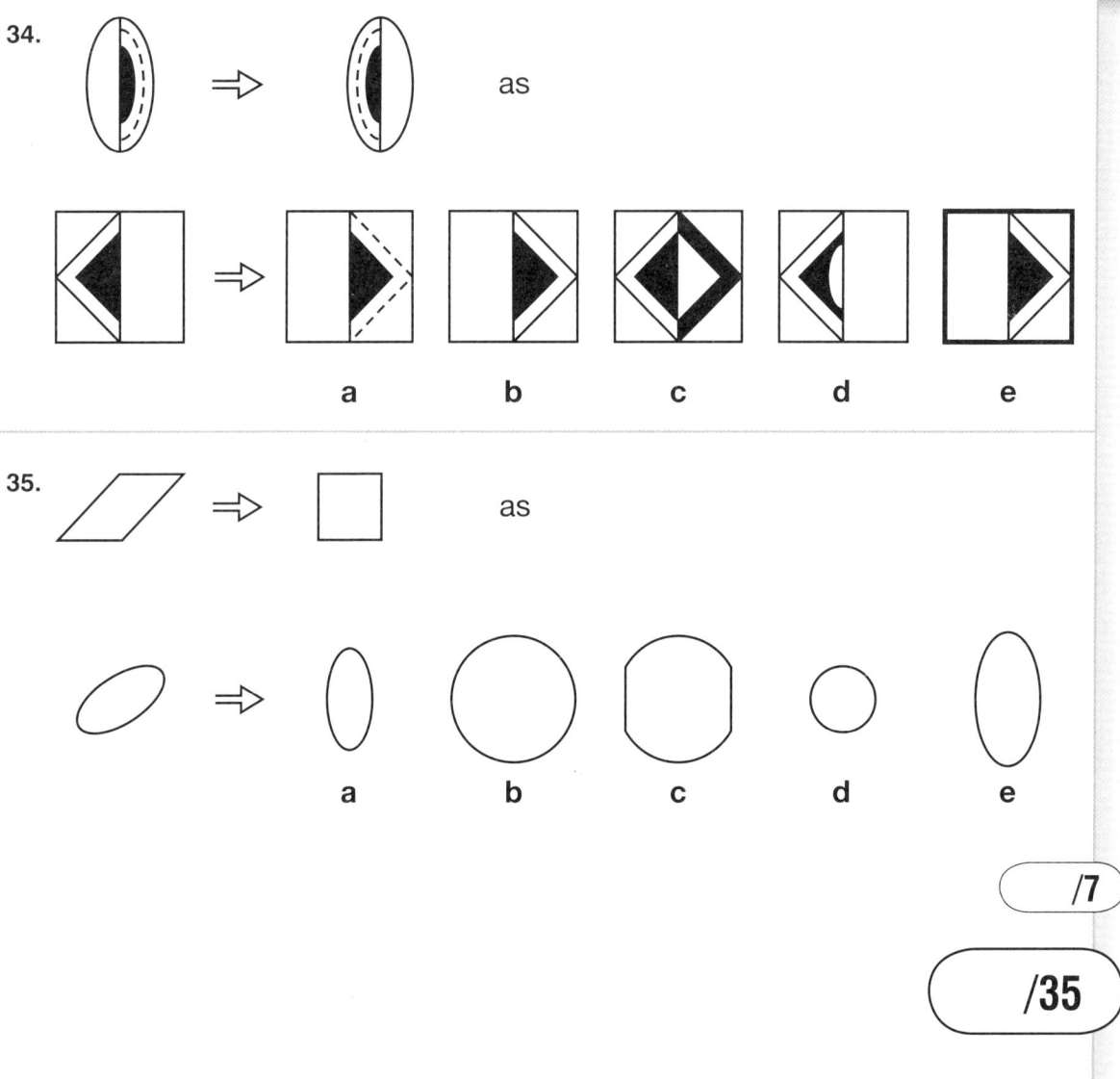

as

35.

as

/7

/35

PAPER 2

Example

Look at the patterns and letter codes to work out the new code. Circle the letter under the code.

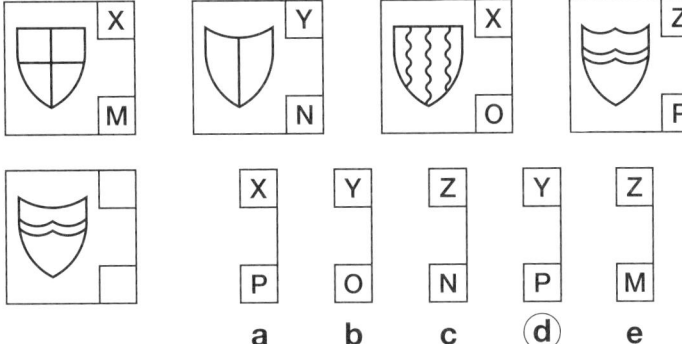

The answer is **d**. X, Y and Z are the codes for the shield shape. M, N, O and P are the codes for the patterns on the shields. In this case, the shield is Y and the pattern is P, so **d** is circled.

Now try these. Look at the patterns and letter codes to work out the new code. Circle the letter under the code.

1.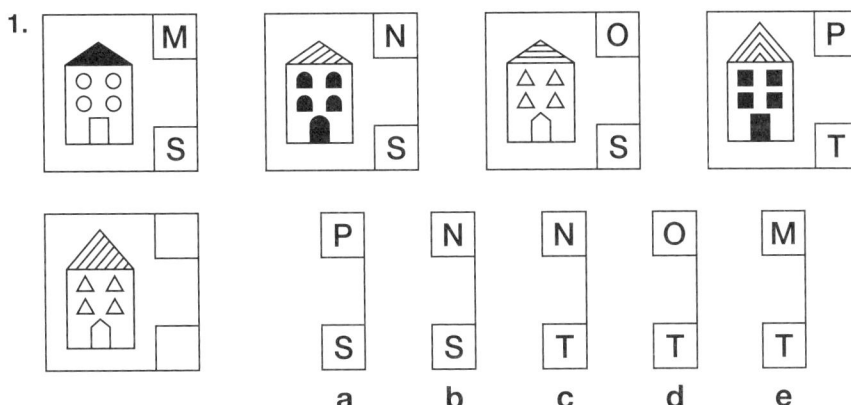

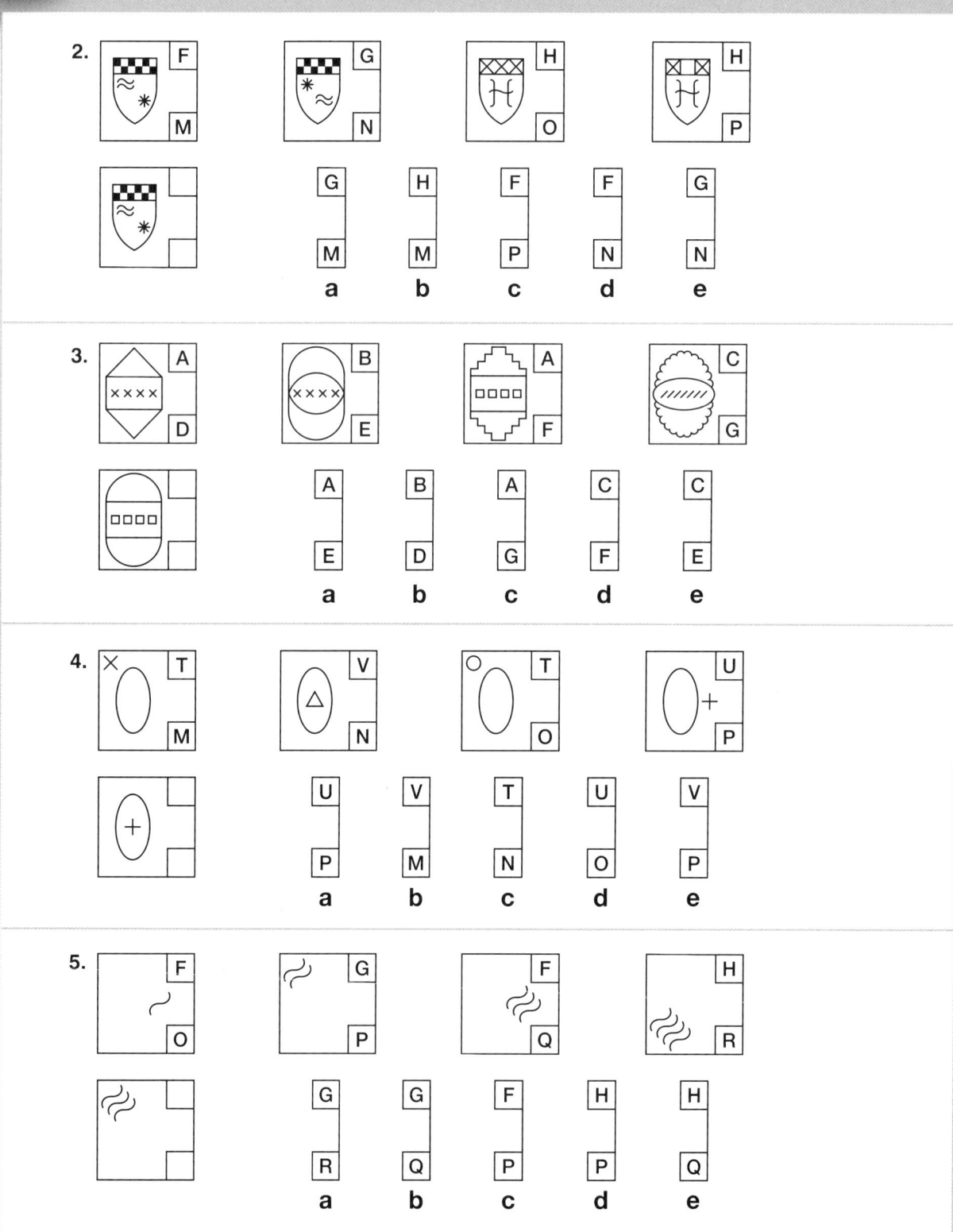

6.

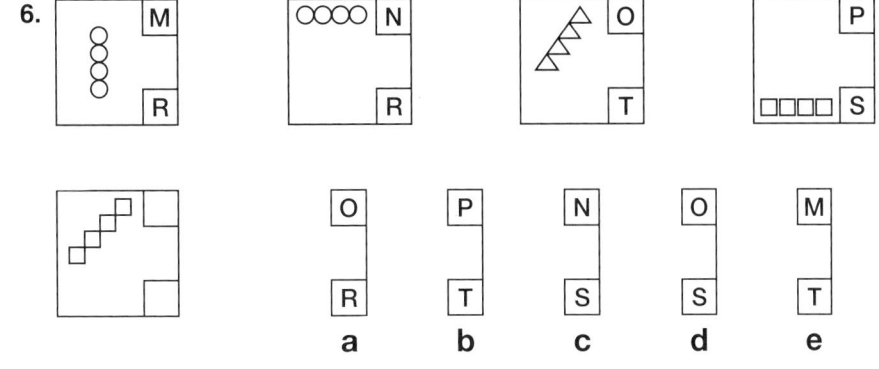

a　　b　　c　　d　　e

7.

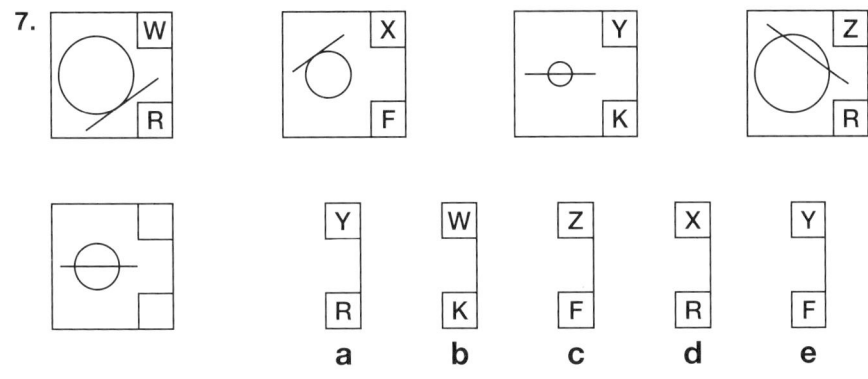

a　　b　　c　　d　　e

/7

Example

Choose the shape or pattern from the right-hand side which belongs to the set on the left-hand side. Circle the letter under it.

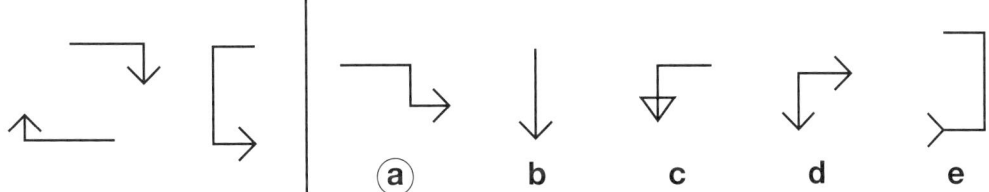

a　　b　　c　　d　　e

The answer is **a** as it is the only one that completes the set.

It cannot be the other shapes because **b** is a straight arrow, **c** has the wrong arrow head, **d** has two arrow heads and in **e**, the arrow is reversed.

Now try these. Choose the shape or pattern from the right-hand side which belongs to the set on the left-hand side. Circle the letter under it.

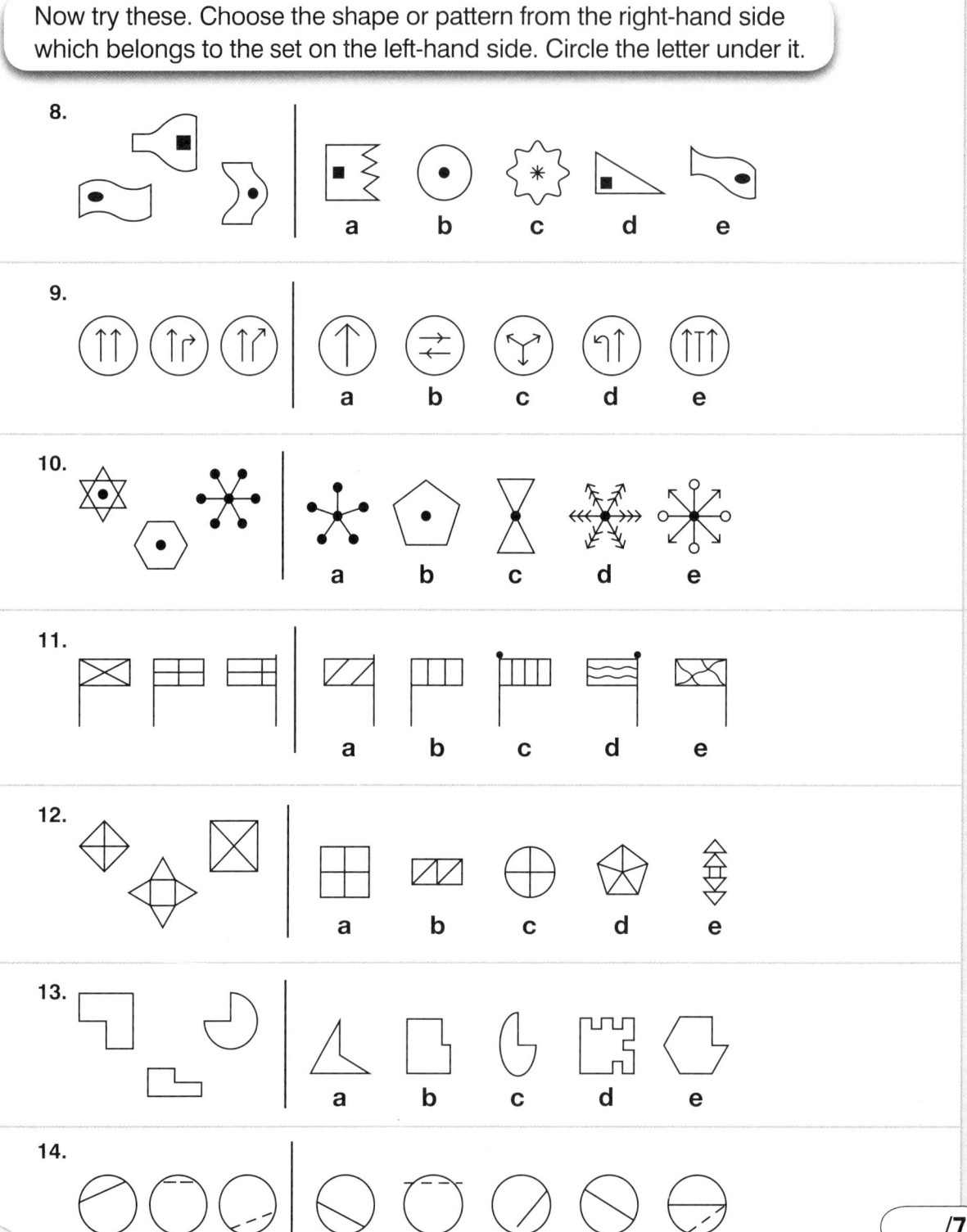

8.

a   b   c   d   e

9.

a   b   c   d   e

10.

a   b   c   d   e

11.

a   b   c   d   e

12.

a   b   c   d   e

13.

a   b   c   d   e

14.

a   b   c   d   e

/7

Example

Find the shape or pattern which completes the sequence. Circle the letter under it.

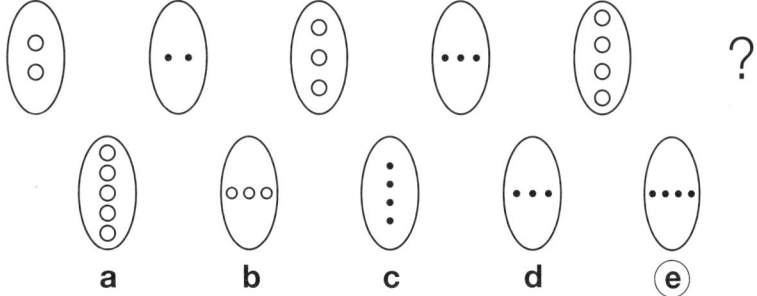

The answer is **e** because the pattern is large circles in a vertical line, followed by the same number of small black circles in a horizontal line.

Now try these. Find the shape or pattern which completes the sequence. Circle the letter under it.

15.

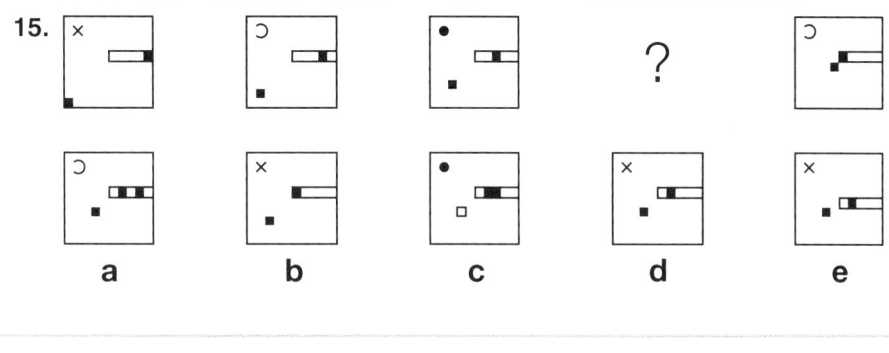

16.

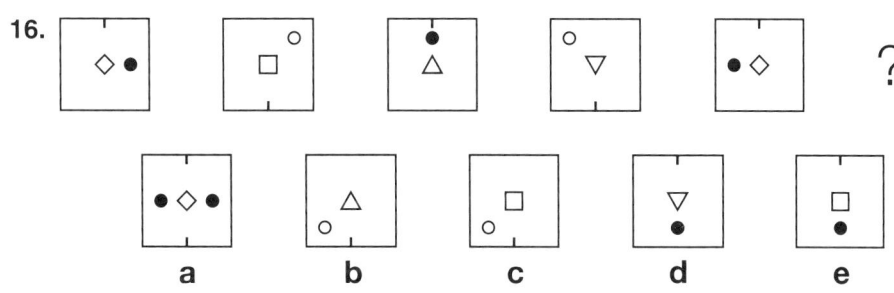

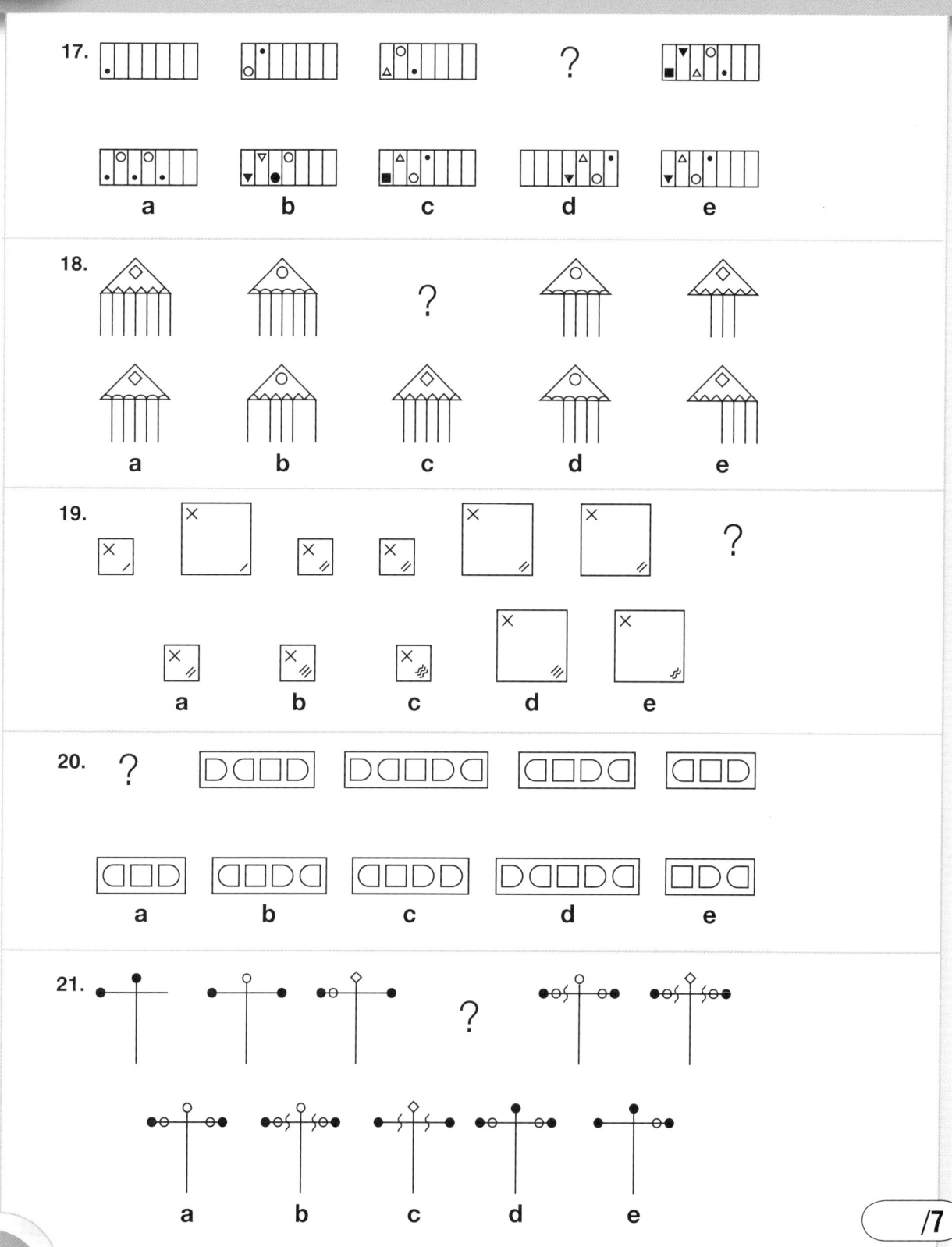

17.

18.

19.

20.

21.

/7

Example

Match the missing part of the second pair in a similar way to the first pair. Circle the letter under the missing part.

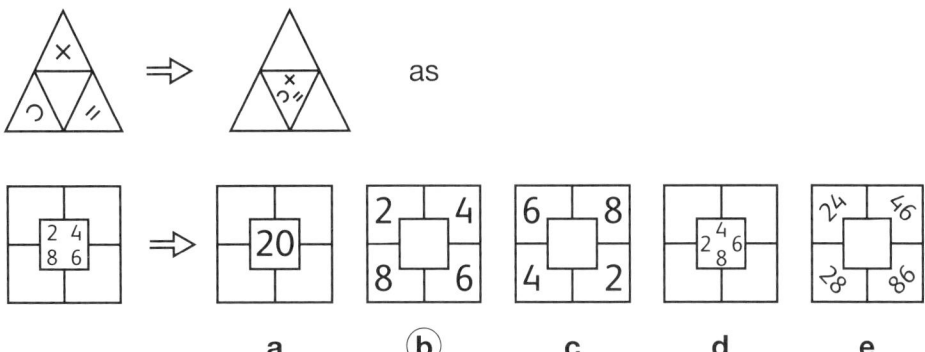

The answer is **b**.

Now try these. Match the missing part of the second pair in a similar way to the first pair. Circle the letter under the missing part.

22.

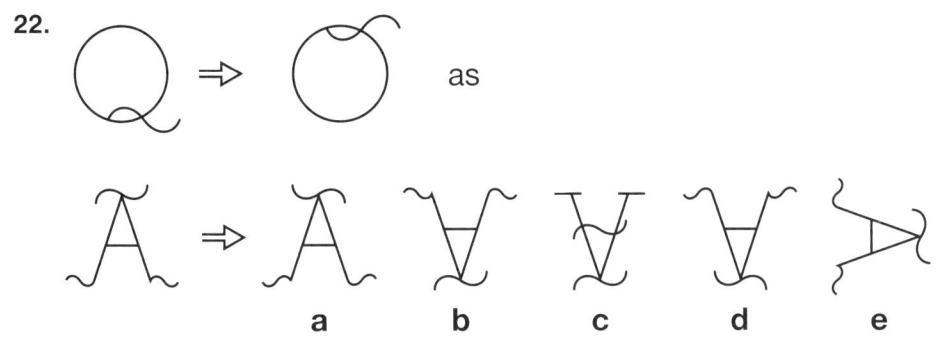

23.

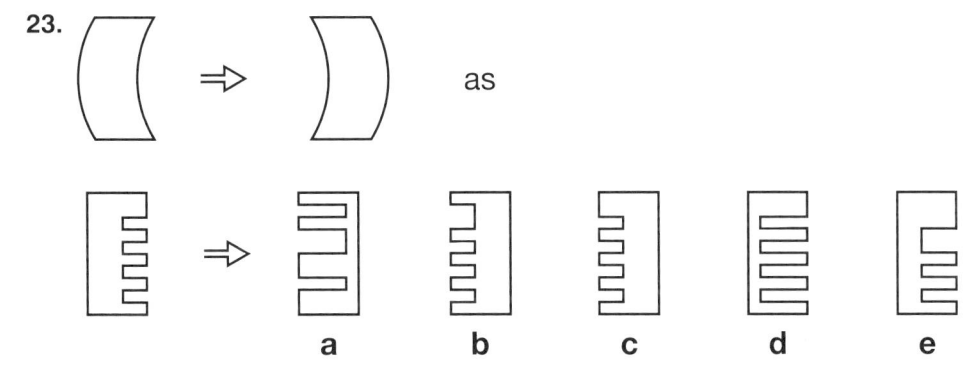

24.  as

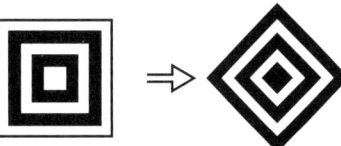    

                           a   b   c   d   e

25. 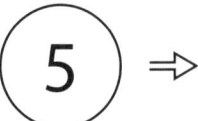 as

 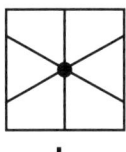 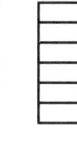

                           a   b   c   d   e

26.   as

                           a   b   c   d   e

27.  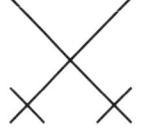 as

  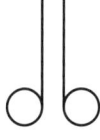

                           a   b   c   d   e

28.

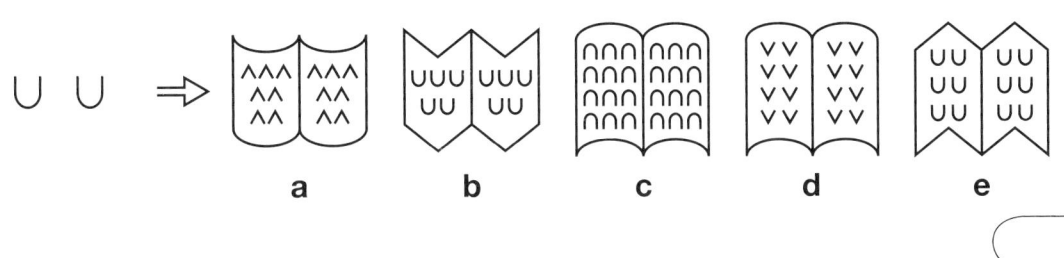

as

a   **b**   **c**   **d**   **e**

/7

Example

Complete the grid by finding the missing square.
Circle the letter under the square.

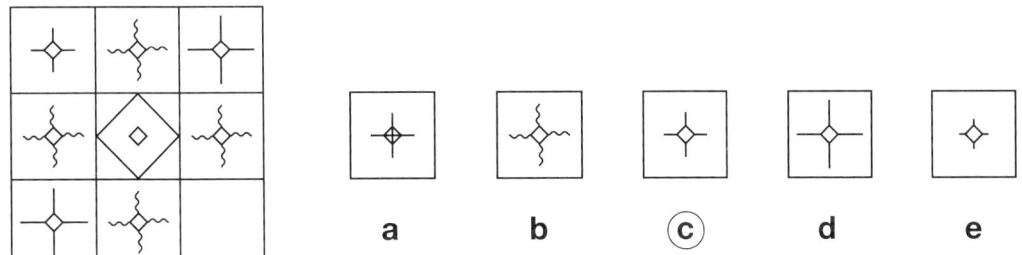

a   **b**   **c**   **d**   **e**

The answer is **c** because the outer squares of the grid are the same on the diagonal.

Now try these. Complete the grid by finding the missing square.
Circle the letter under the square.

29.

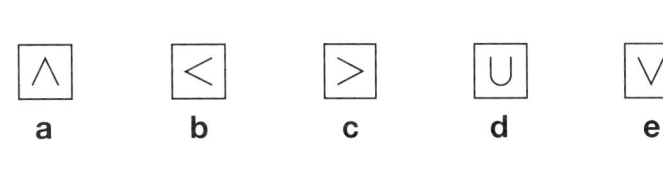

a   **b**   **c**   **d**   **e**

30.

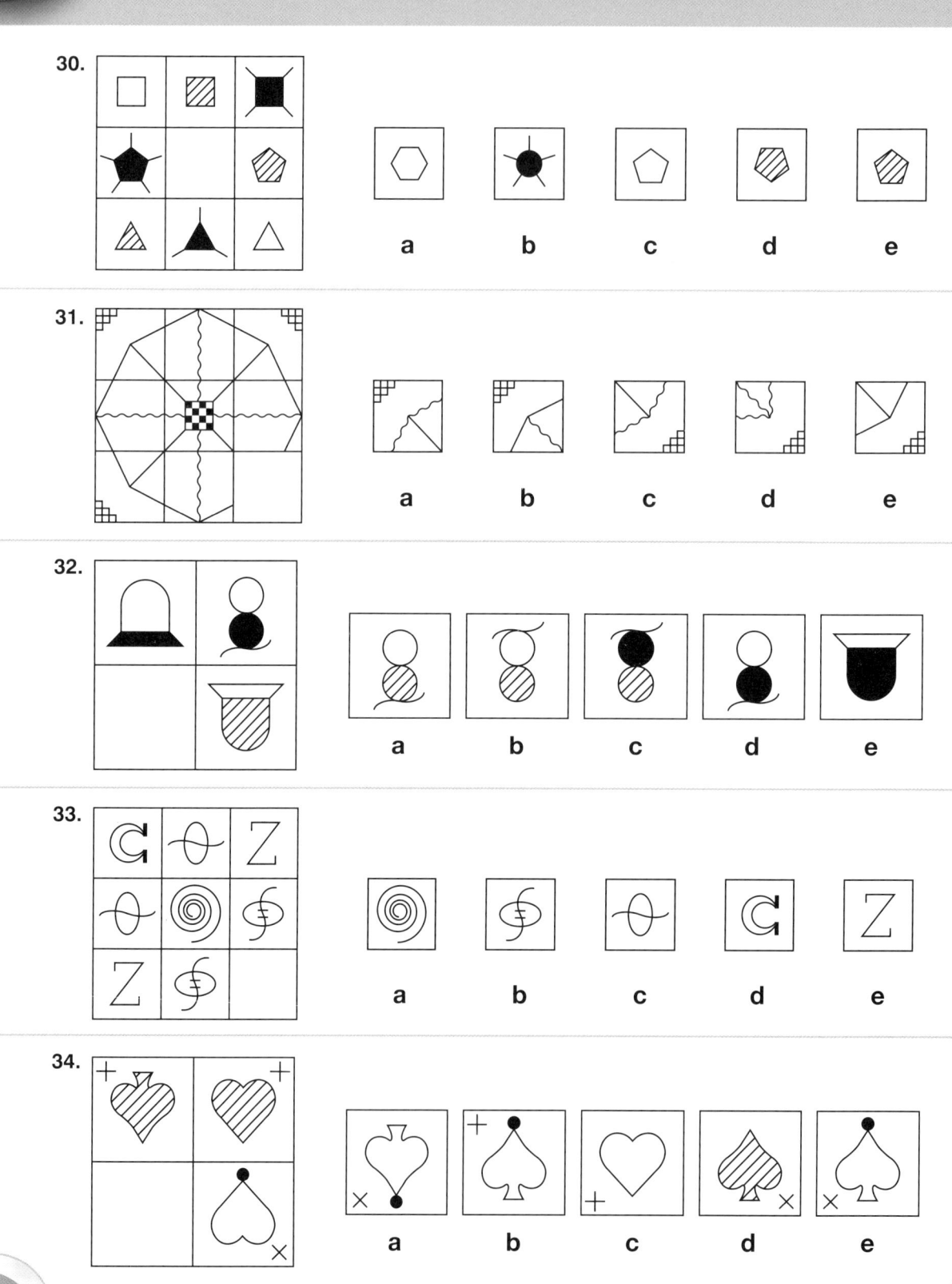

a b c d e

31.

a b c d e

32.

a b c d e

33.

a b c d e

34.

a b c d e

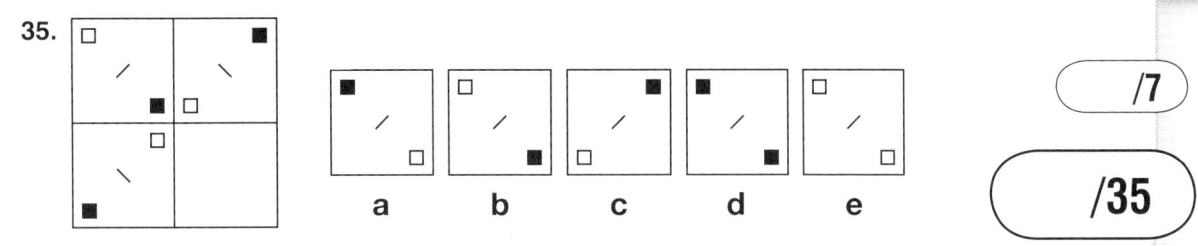

35.

/7

/35

PAPER 3

Example

Find the shape or pattern which completes the sequence.
Circle the letter under it.

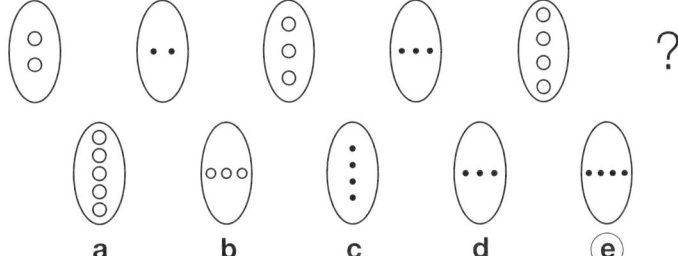

The answer is **e** because the pattern is large circles in a vertical line, followed by the same number of small black circles in a horizontal line.

Now try these. Find the shape or pattern which completes the sequence. Circle the letter under it.

1.

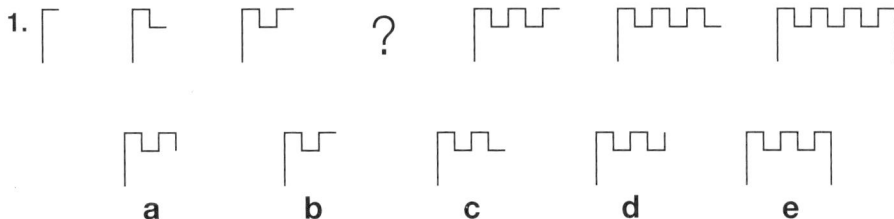

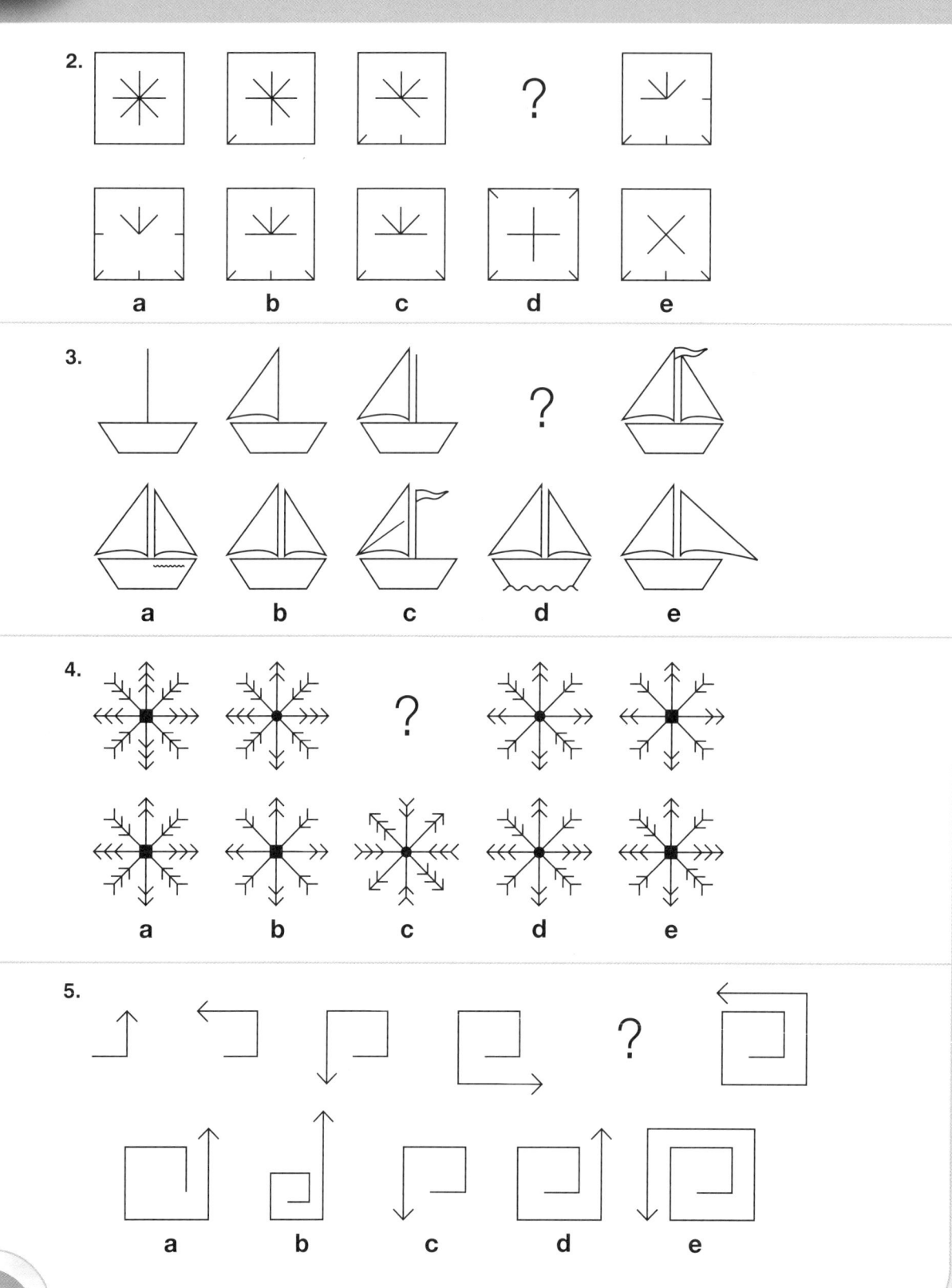

2.

a   b   c   d   e

3.

a   b   c   d   e

4.

a   b   c   d   e

5.

a   b   c   d   e

6.

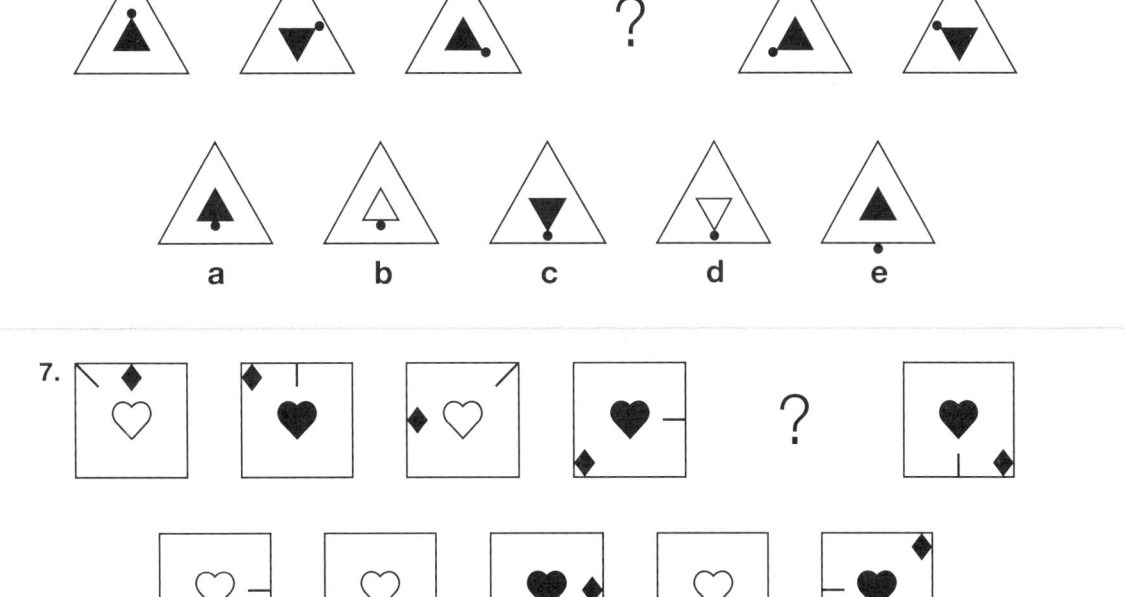

7.

Example

> Look at the patterns and letter codes to work out the new code. Circle the letter under the code.

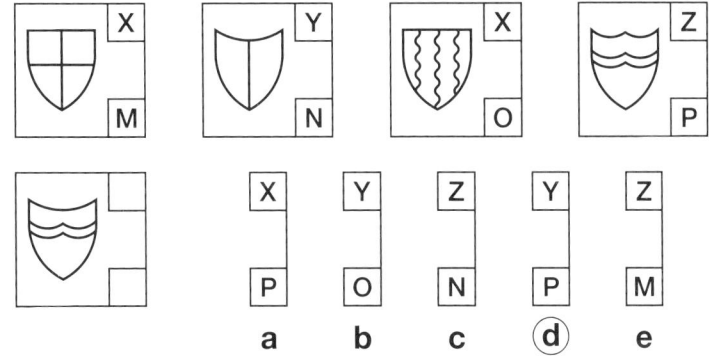

The answer is **d**. X, Y and Z are the codes for the shield shape. M, N, O and P are the codes for the patterns on the shields. In this case, the shield is Y and the pattern is P, so **d** is circled.

Now try these. Look at the patterns and letter codes to work out the new code. Circle the letter under the code.

8.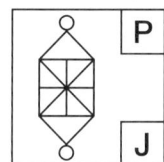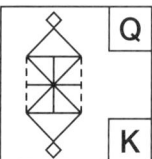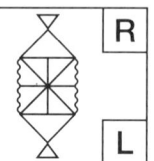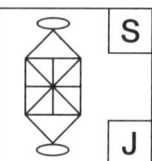

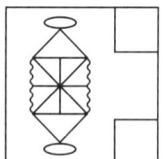

P	S	R	S	Q
L	K	J	L	J
a	b	c	d	e

9.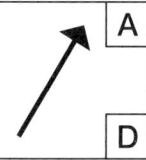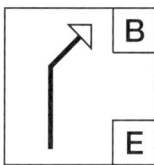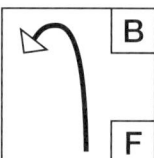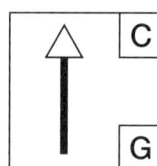

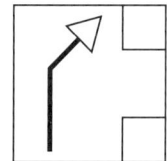

C	B	C	A	B
D	D	E	F	G
a	b	c	d	e

10.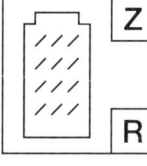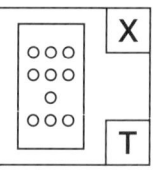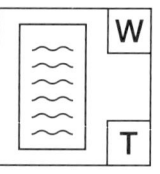

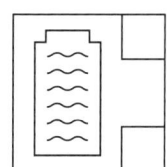

W	X	Y	Z	W
S	S	R	T	R
a	b	c	d	e

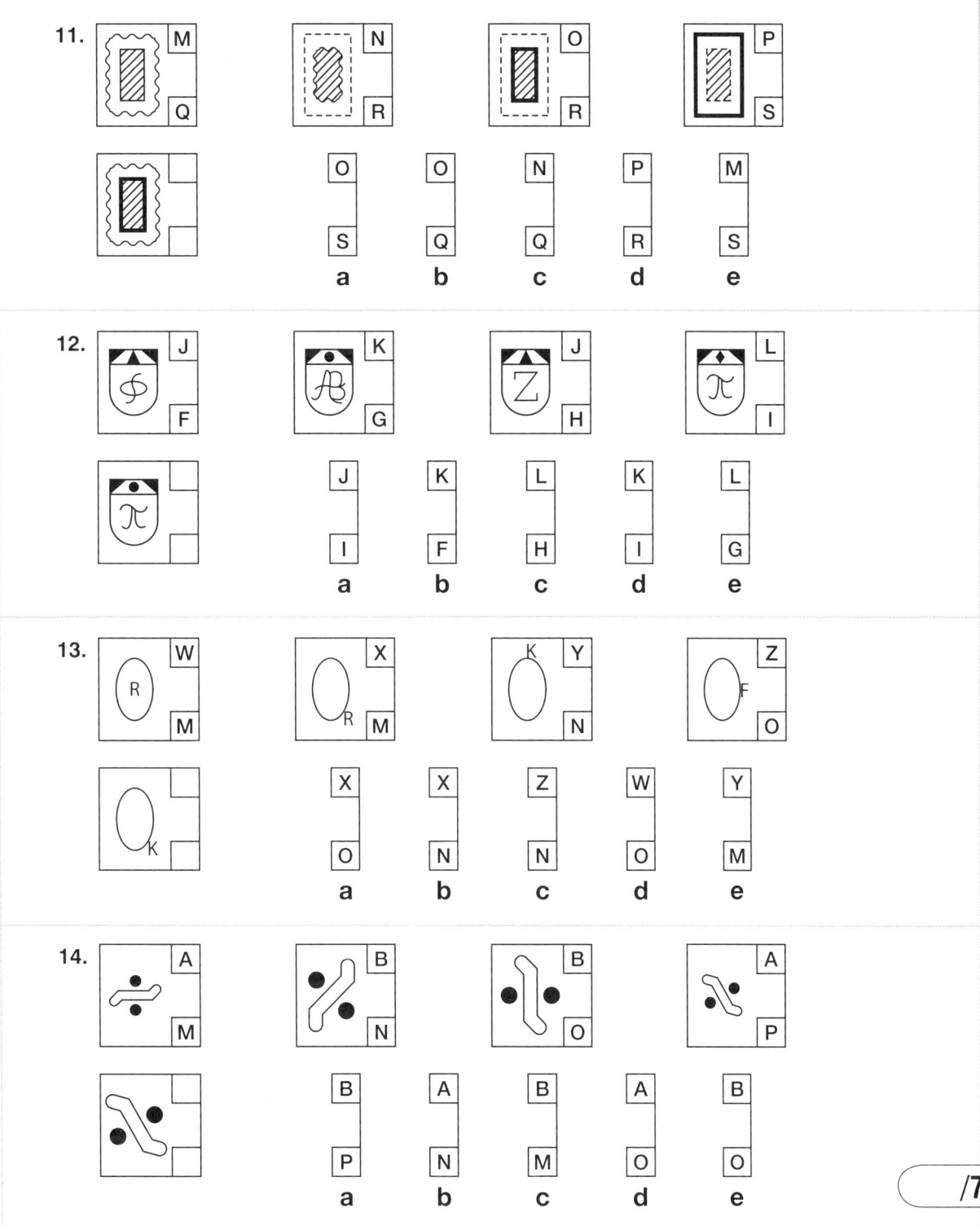

/7

Example

Choose the shape or pattern from the right-hand side which belongs to the set on the left-hand side. Circle the letter under it.

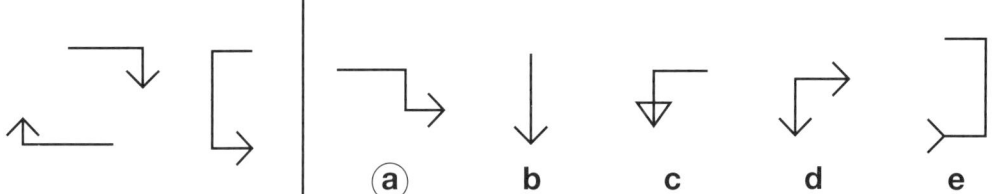

The answer is **a** as it is the only one that completes the set.

It cannot be the other shapes because **b** is a straight arrow, **c** has the wrong arrow head, **d** has two arrow heads and in **e**, the arrow is reversed.

Now try these. Choose the shape or pattern from the right-hand side which belongs to the set on the left-hand side. Circle the letter under it.

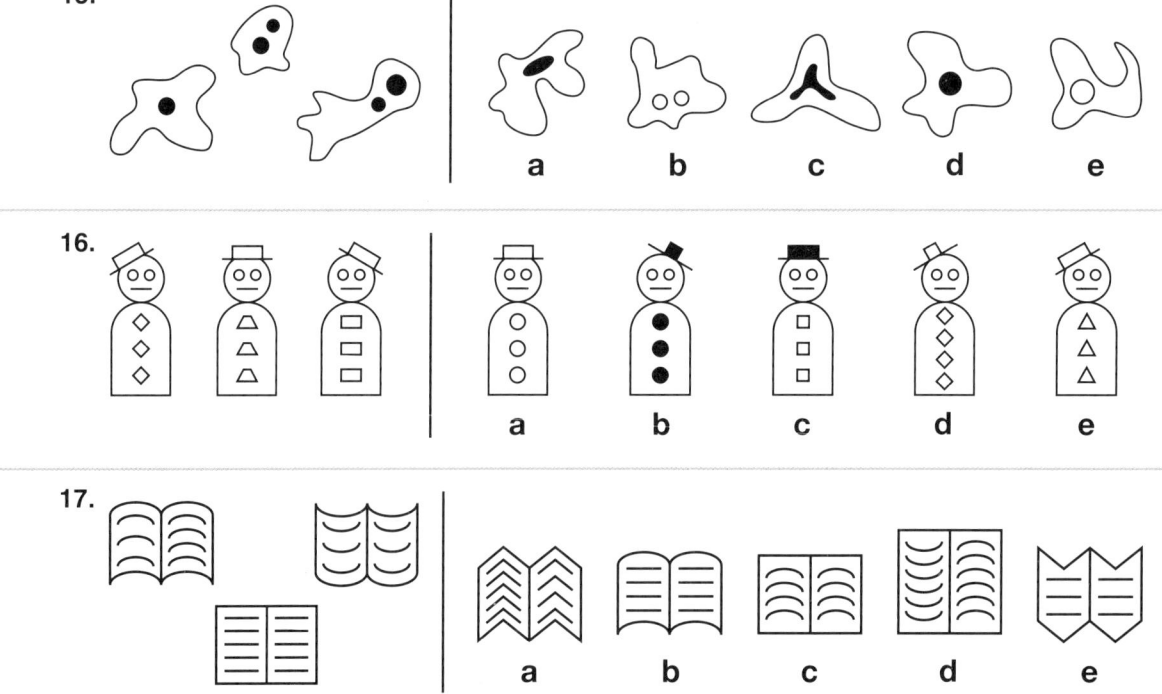

18.

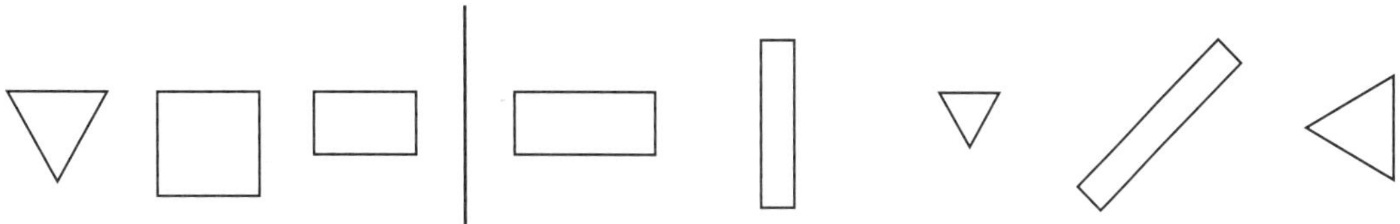

a   b   c   d   e

19.

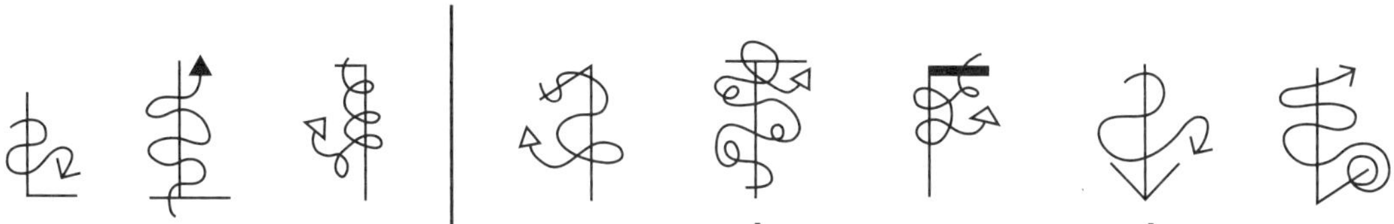

a   b   c   d   e

20.

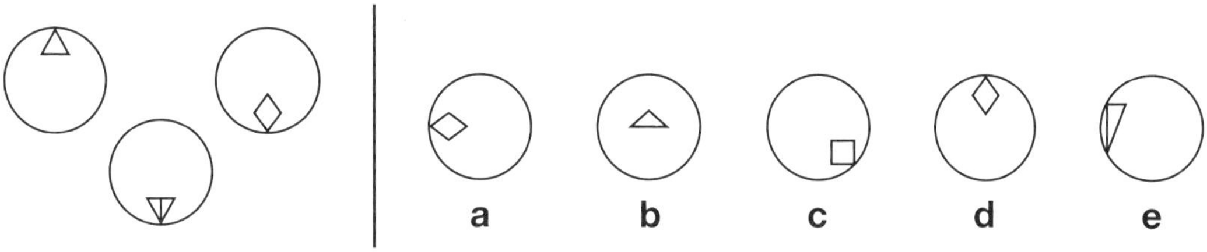

a   b   c   d   e

21.

a   b   c   d   e

/7

Example

> Complete the grid by finding the missing square.
> Circle the letter under the square.

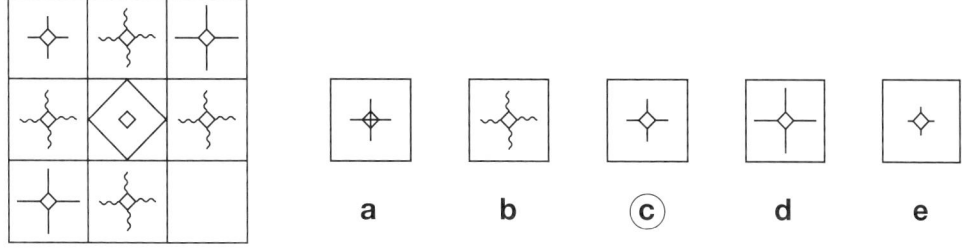

a   b   c   d   e

The answer is **c** because the outer squares of the grid are the same on the diagonal.

Now try these. Complete the grid by finding the missing square.
Circle the letter under the square.

22.

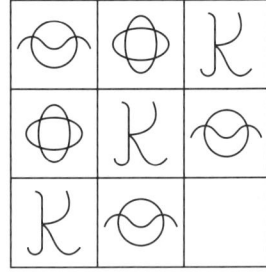

a   b   c   d   e

23.

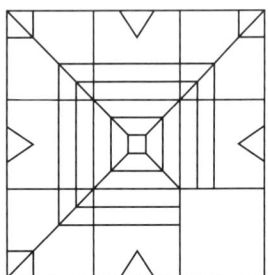

a   b   c   d   e

24.

a   b   c   d   e

25.

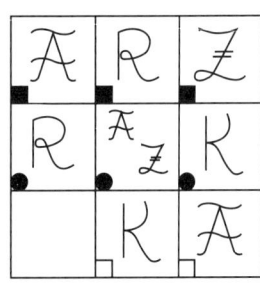

a   b   c   d   e

26.

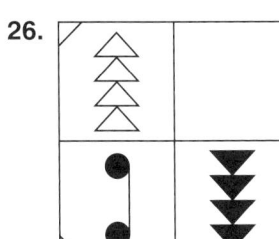 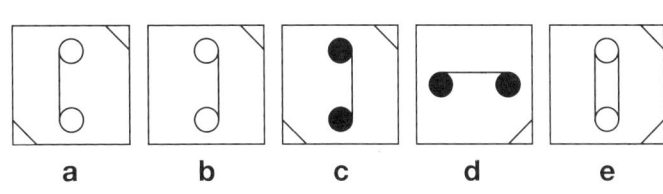

a   b   c   d   e

27.

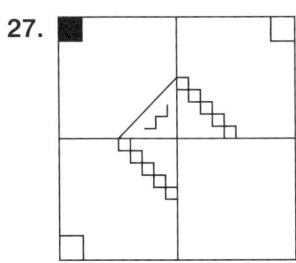 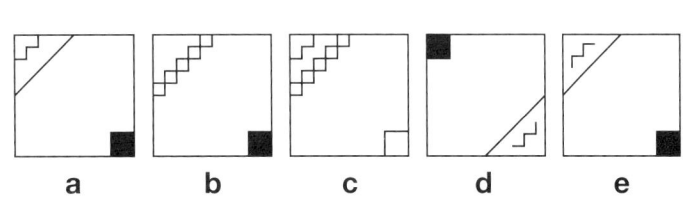

a   b   c   d   e

28.

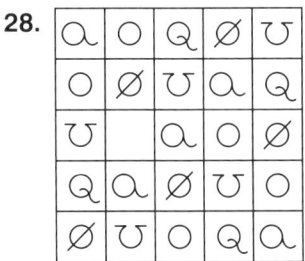 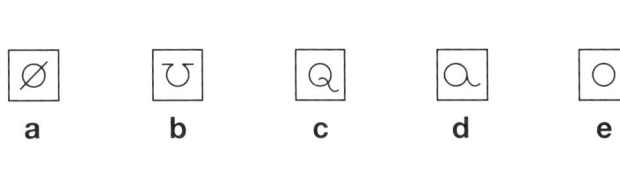

a   b   c   d   e

Example

> Match the missing part of the second pair in a similar way to the first pair. Circle the letter under the missing part.

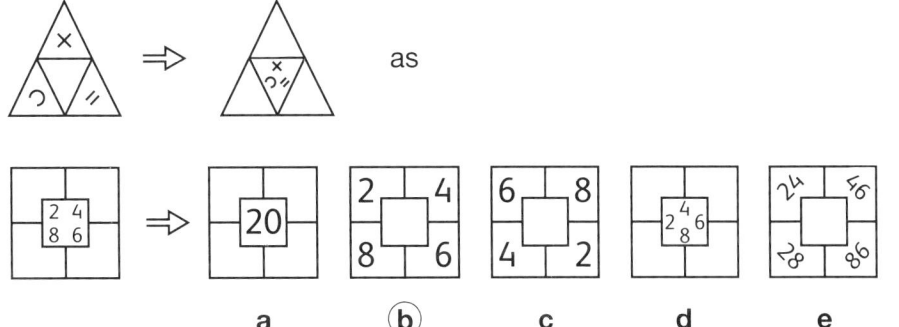

a   (b)   c   d   e

The answer is **b**.

Now try these. Match the missing part of the second pair in a similar way to the first pair. Circle the letter under the missing part.

29. 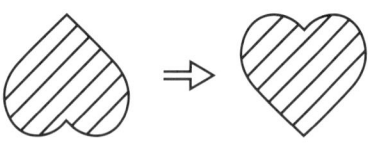 as

  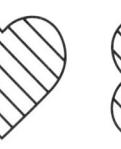 

    a   b   c   d   e

30.  as

   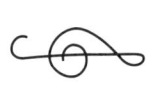

    a   b   c   d   e

31.  as

    a   b   c   d   e

Success

Assessment Papers

Non-Verbal Reasoning

age 10 – 11

Answer booklet

Answer booklet: Non-Verbal Reasoning age 10–11

Paper 1
1. c
2. b
3. e
4. a
5. a
6. e
7. d
8. d
9. d
10. e
11. a
12. a
13. c
14. b
15. b
16. d
17. e
18. a
19. c
20. e
21. c
22. b
23. d
24. c
25. a
26. d
27. c
28. d
29. e
30. d

31. e
32. b
33. c
34. b
35. d

Paper 2
1. d
2. d
3. a
4. e
5. b
6. d
7. e
8. e
9. d
10. d
11. c
12. b
13. c
14. a
15. d
16. c
17. e
18. c
19. b
20. a
21. d
22. d
23. c

24. e
25. b
26. e
27. b
28. c
29. a
30. c
31. e
32. b
33. d
34. e
35. a

Paper 3
1. c
2. b
3. b
4. e
5. d
6. c
7. d
8. d
9. c
10. e
11. b
12. d
13. b
14. a
15. d
16. e

17. a
18. e
19. b
20. d
21. a
22. c
23. d
24. b
25. e
26. b
27. e
28. c
29. d
30. c
31. d
32. e
33. a
34. b
35. b

Paper 4
1. d
2. e
3. b
4. d
5. c
6. a
7. b
8. e
9. d
10. a
11. c
12. d
13. e

14. c
15. a
16. d
17. c
18. e
19. b
20. d
21. a
22. c
23. c
24. d
25. e
26. b
27. d
28. a
29. d
30. c
31. d
32. a
33. e
34. c
35. a

Paper 5
1. c
2. e
3. d
4. c
5. b
6. e
7. b
8. a
9. c
10. e

11. d
12. c
13. a
14. d
15. b
16. c
17. d
18. a
19. e
20. d
21. a
22. d
23. e
24. c
25. b
26. d
27. a
28. d
29. c
30. b
31. e
32. d
33. e
34. a
35. b

Paper 6
1. d
2. c
3. a
4. d
5. e
6. c
7. b

8. c	**18.** b	**28.** e
9. d	**19.** c	**29.** d
10. b	**20.** b	**30.** c
11. e	**21.** e	**31.** e
12. b	**22.** a	**32.** a
13. d	**23.** e	**33.** d
14. a	**24.** c	**34.** b
15. d	**25.** d	**35.** c
16. e	**26.** c	
17. c	**27.** c	

32.

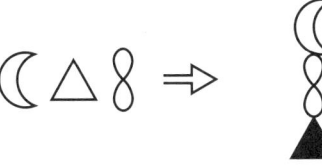  as

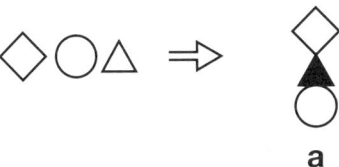 

     a   **b**   **c**   **d**   **e**

33.

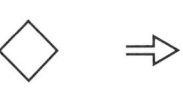  as

     a   **b**   **c**   **d**   **e**

34.

 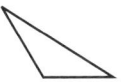 as

   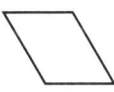 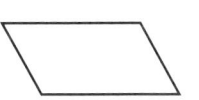  

     a   **b**   **c**   **d**   **e**

35. 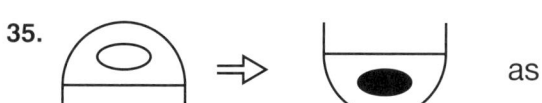 as

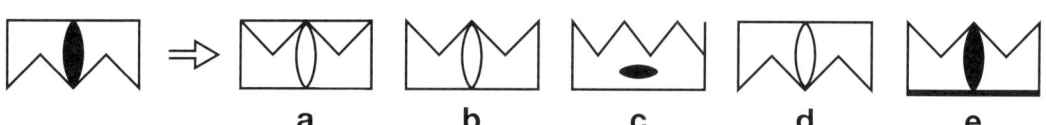

/7

/35

PAPER 4

Example

Complete the grid by finding the missing square.
Circle the letter under the square.

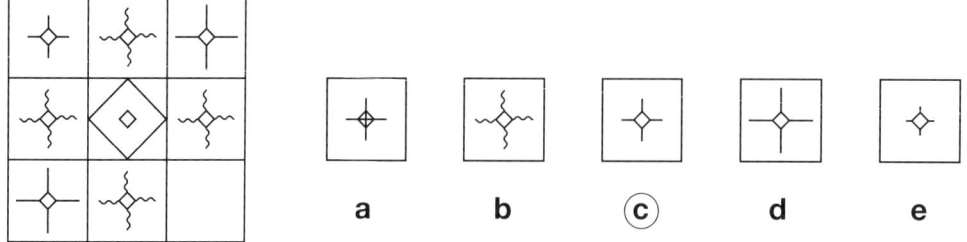

The answer is **c** because the outer squares of the grid are the same on the diagonal.

Now try these. Complete the grid by finding the missing square.
Circle the letter under the square.

1.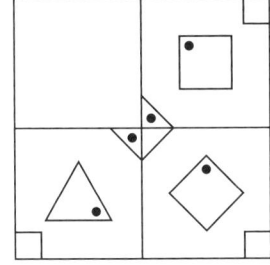

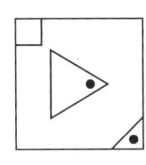 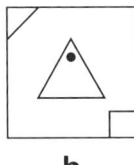 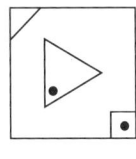 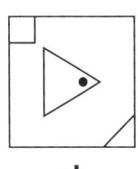 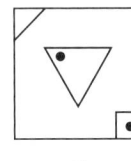

   a   b   c   d   e

2.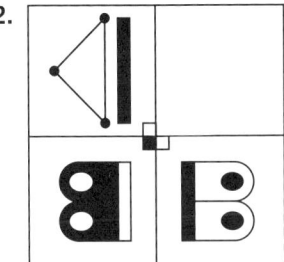

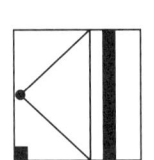 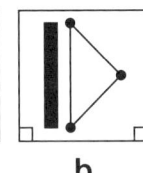  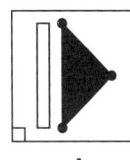 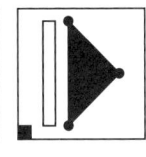

   a   b   c   d   e

3.

e	E	∈	F	e
E	∈	e	e	F
∈	e		e	E
F	e	e	E	∈
e	F	E	∈	e

  e   F   E   e   ∈

  a   b   c   d   e

4.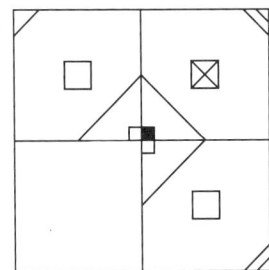

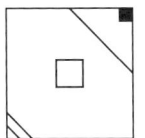 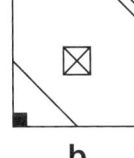 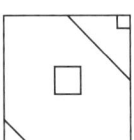 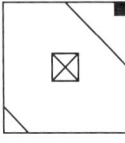 

   a   b   c   d   e

5.

a   b   c   d   e

6.

a   b   c   d   e

7.

a   b   c   d   e

Example

Match the missing part of the second pair in a similar way to the first pair. Circle the letter under the missing part.

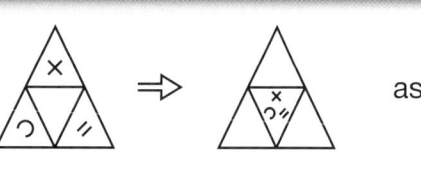   as

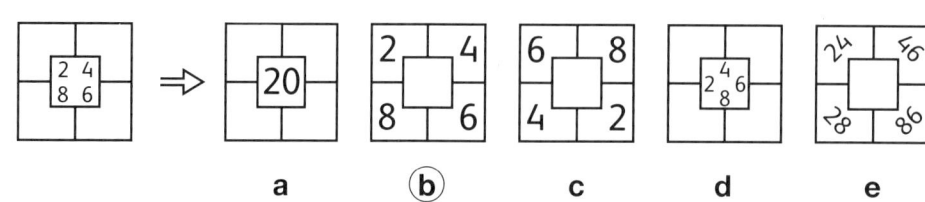

a   (b)   c   d   e

The answer is **b**.

Now try these. Match the missing part of the second pair in a similar way to the first pair. Circle the letter under the missing part.

8.

       a   b   c   d   e

9.

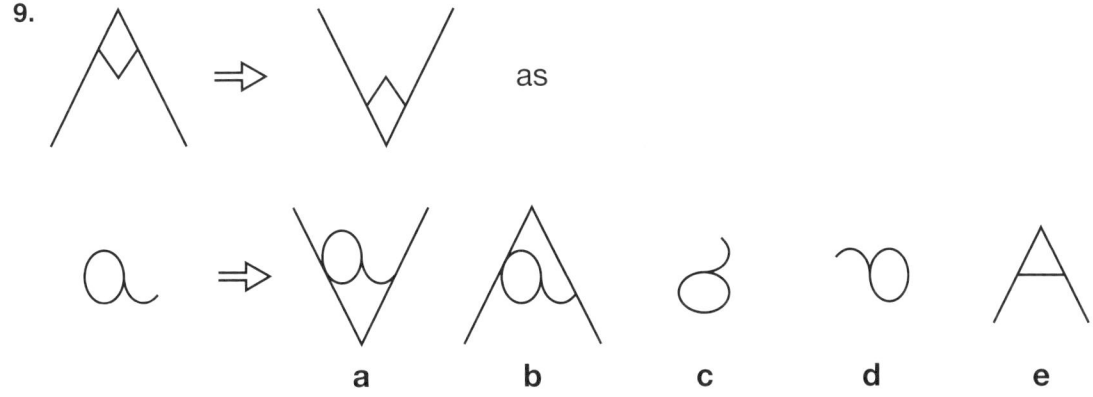

       a   b   c   d   e

10.

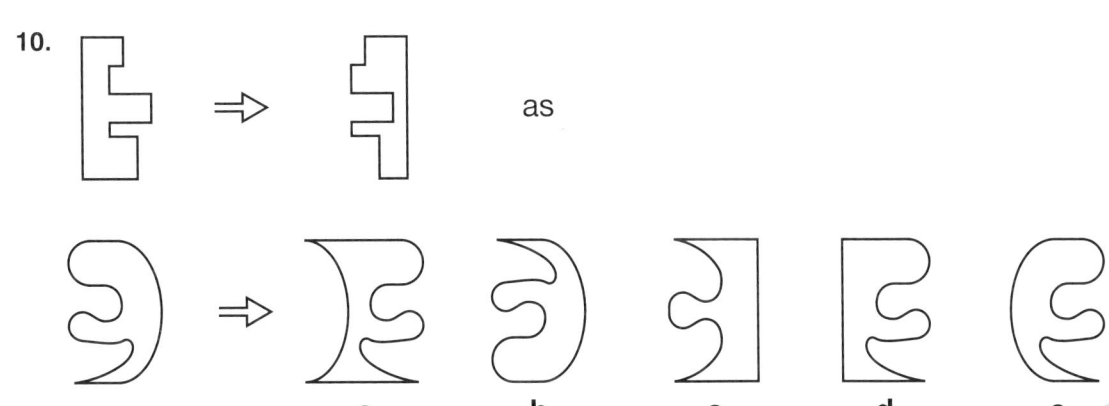

       a   b   c   d   e

11.

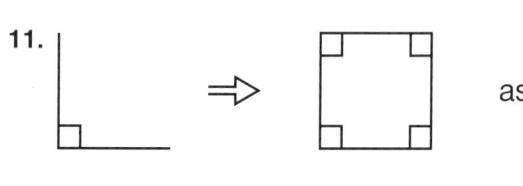

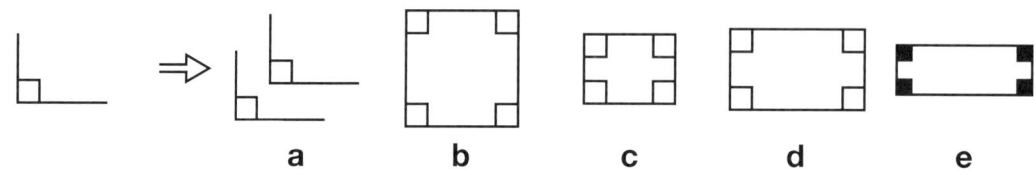

a   b   c   d   e

12.

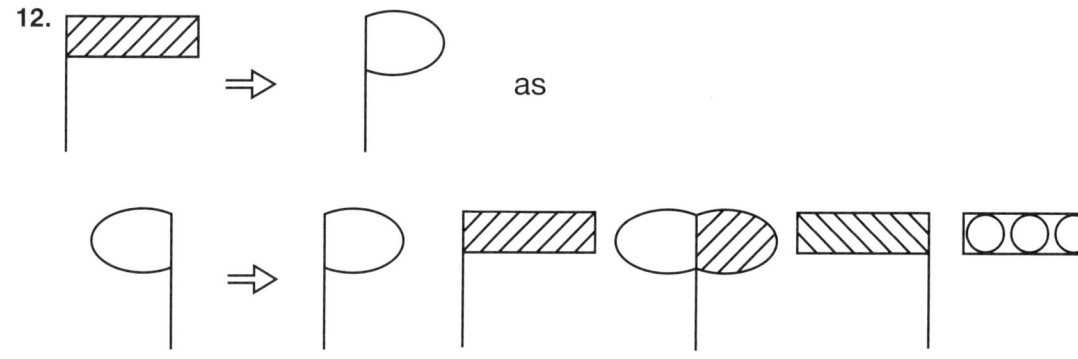

a   b   c   d   e

13.

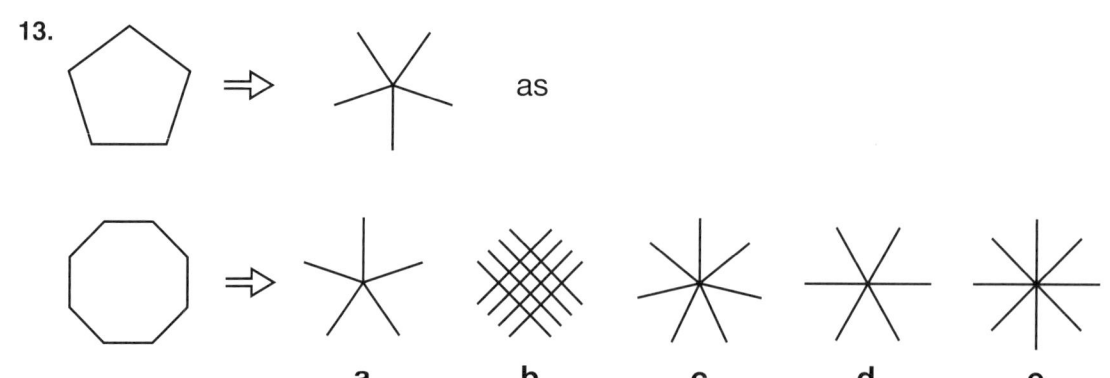

a   b   c   d   e

14.

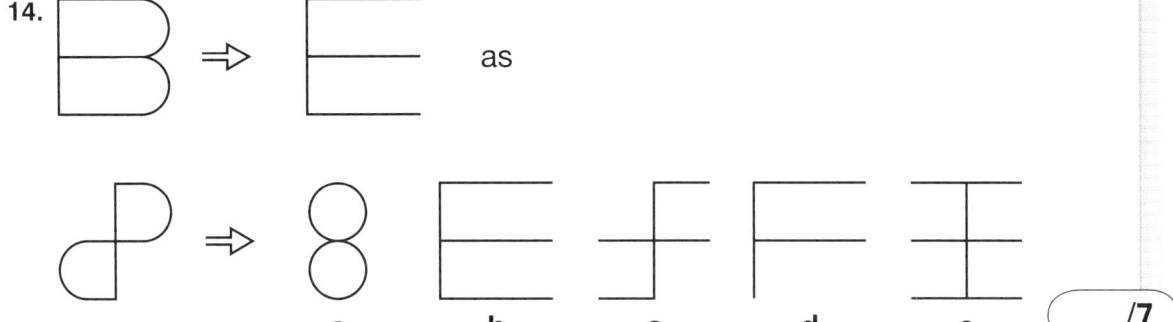

a b c d e

/7

Example

Look at the patterns and letter codes to work out
the new code. Circle the letter under the code.

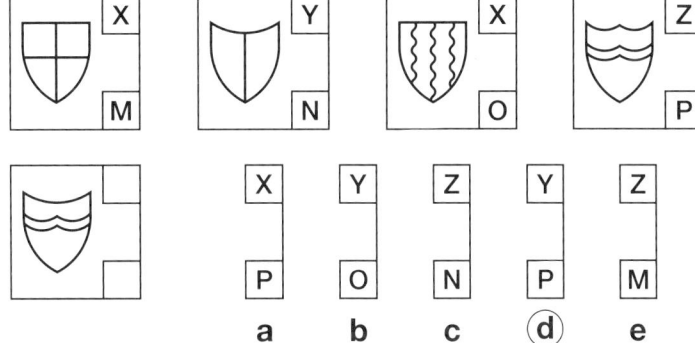

a b c d e

The answer is **d**. X, Y and Z are the codes for the shield shape. M, N, O and P are the codes
for the patterns on the shields. In this case, the shield is Y and the pattern is P, so **d** is circled.

Now try these. Look at the patterns and letter codes to work out the
new code. Circle the letter under the code.

15.

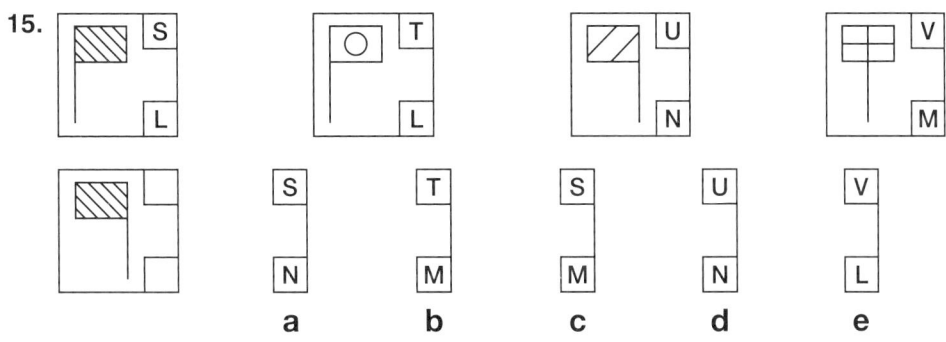

a b c d e

16.

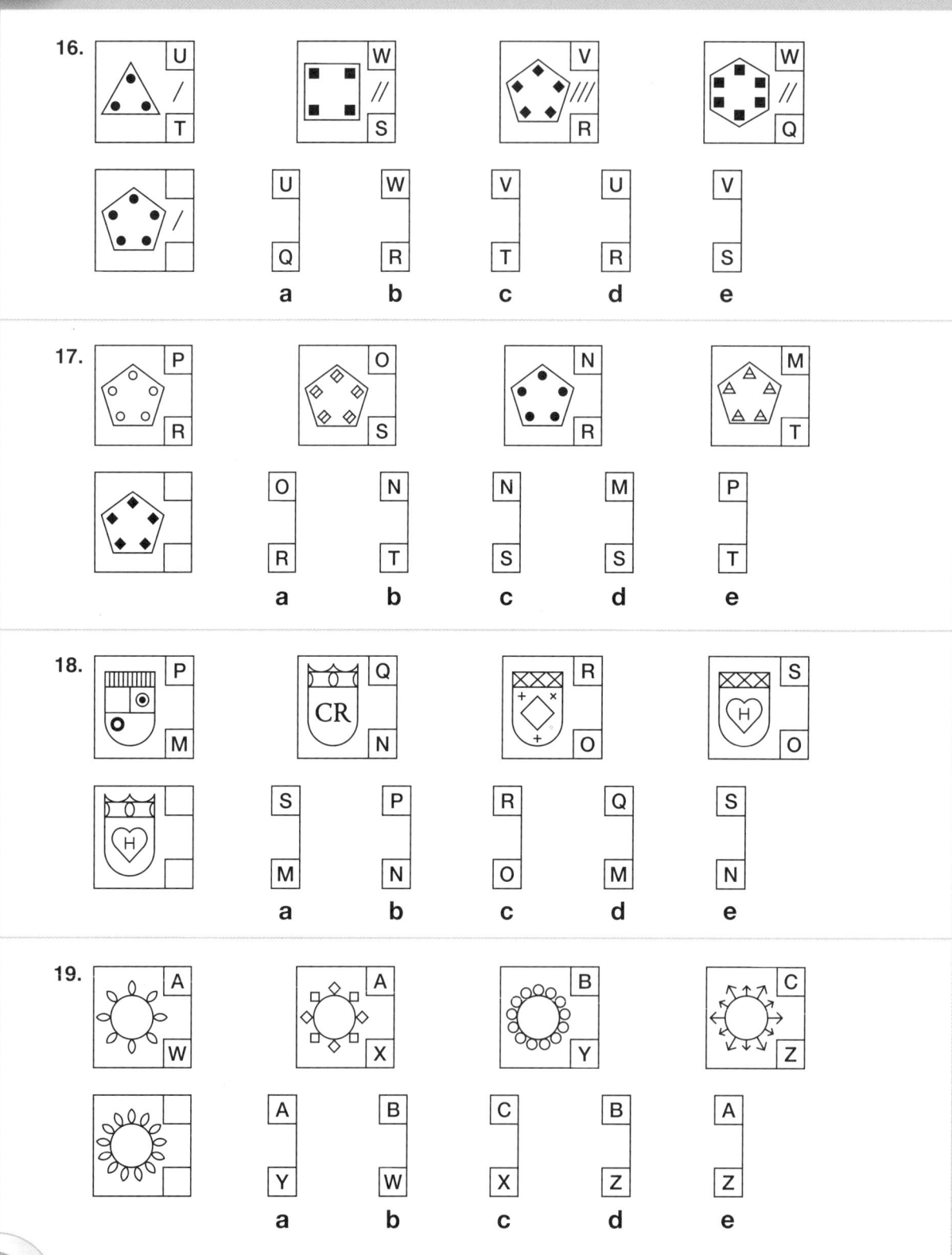

17.

18.

19.

20.

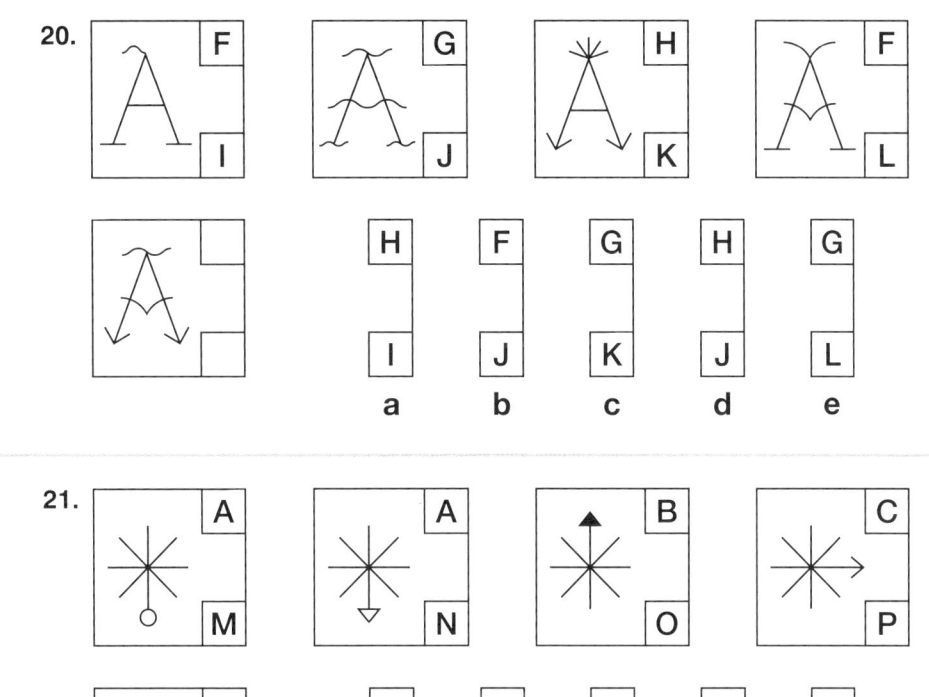

H	F	G	H	G
I	J	K	J	L
a	b	c	d	e

21.

C	A	B	C	B
M	P	N	O	M
a	b	c	d	e

/7

Example

Choose the shape or pattern from the right-hand side which belongs to the set on the left-hand side. Circle the letter under it.

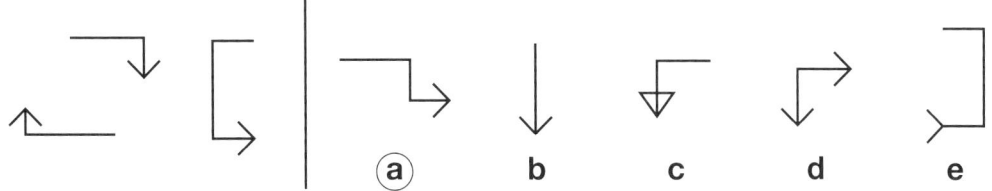

a   b   c   d   e

The answer is **a** as it is the only one that completes the set.

It cannot be the other shapes because **b** is a straight arrow, **c** has the wrong arrow head, **d** has two arrow heads and in **e**, the arrow is reversed.

Now try these. Choose the shape or pattern from the right-hand side which belongs to the set on the left-hand side. Circle the letter under it.

22.

a   b   c   d   e

23.

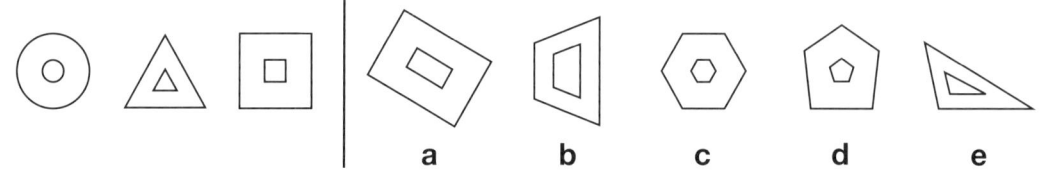

a   b   c   d   e

24.

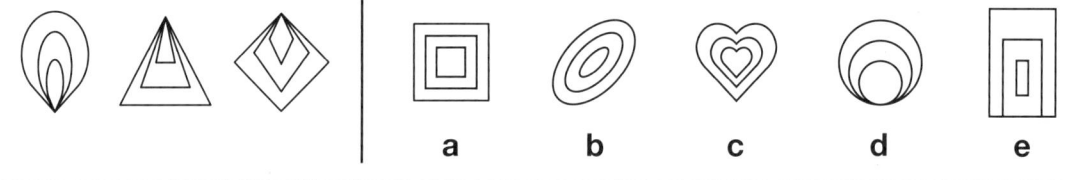

a   b   c   d   e

25.

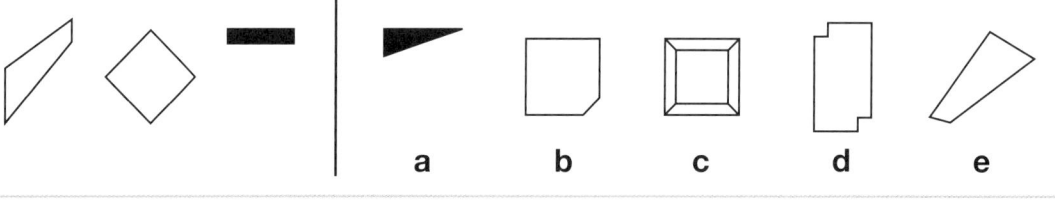

a   b   c   d   e

26.

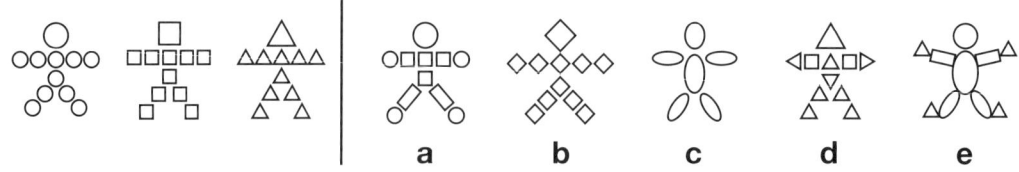

a   b   c   d   e

27.

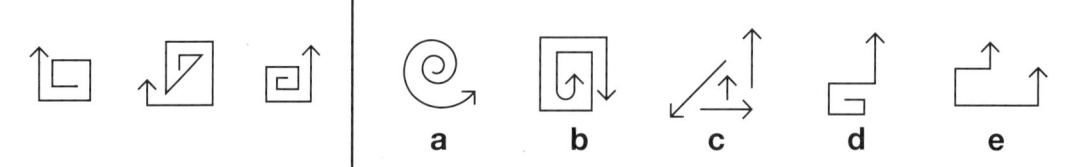

a   b   c   d   e

28.

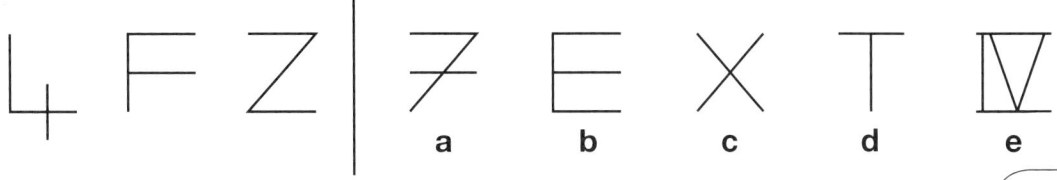

                      a   **b**   **c**   **d**   **e**

/7

Example

Find the shape or pattern which completes the sequence.
Circle the letter under it.

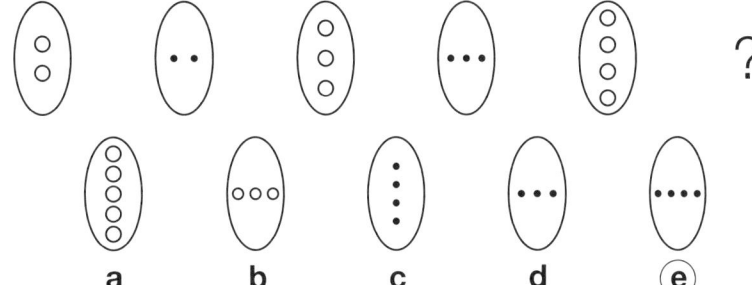

        a   **b**   **c**   **d**   **e**

The answer is **e** because the pattern is large circles in a vertical line, followed by the same number of small black circles in a horizontal line.

Now try these. Find the shape or pattern which completes the sequence. Circle the letter under it.

29.

 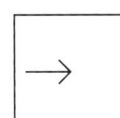 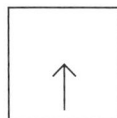 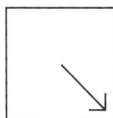

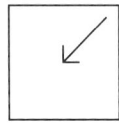 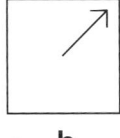 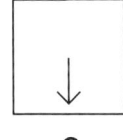  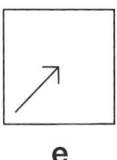

    a   **b**   **c**   **d**   **e**

30.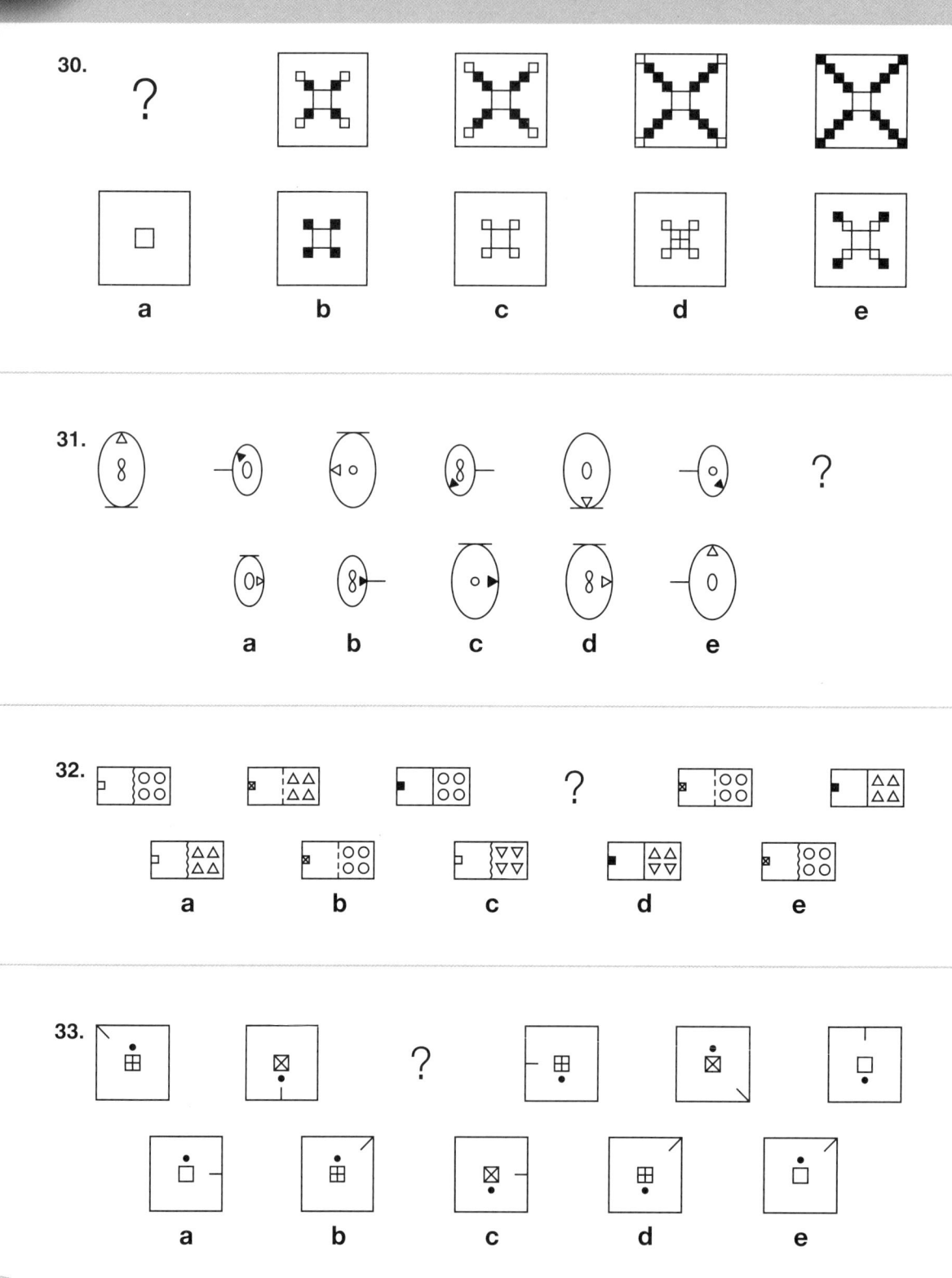

31.

32.

33.

34.

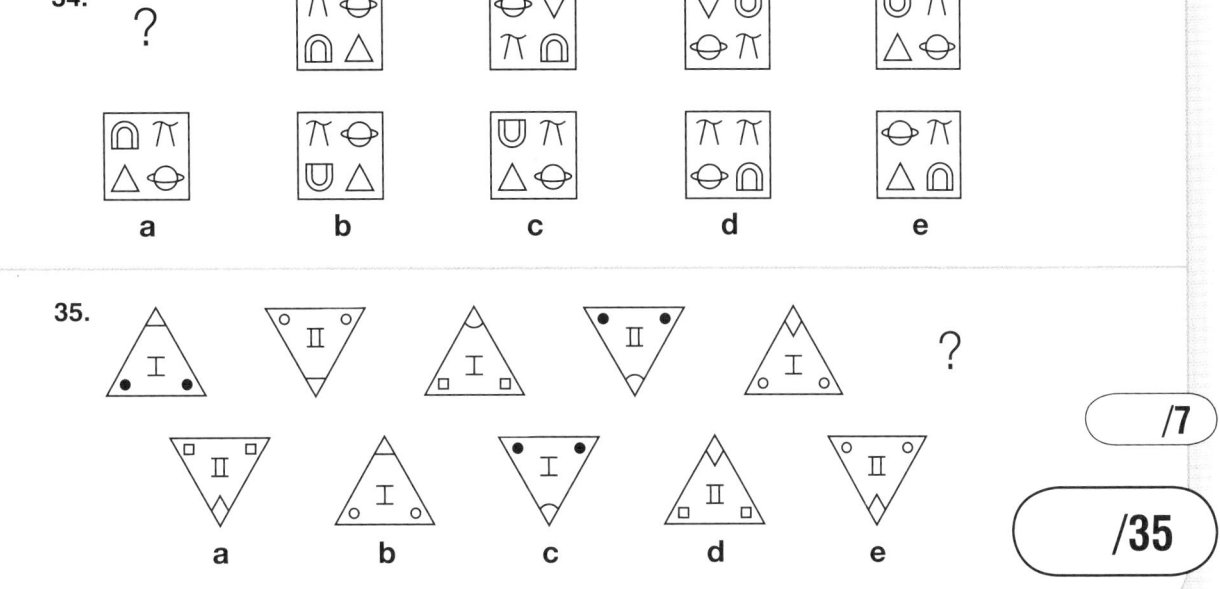

a **b** **c** **d** **e**

35.

?

a **b** **c** **d** **e**

/7

/35

PAPER 5

Example

Match the missing part of the second pair in a similar way to the first pair. Circle the letter under the missing part.

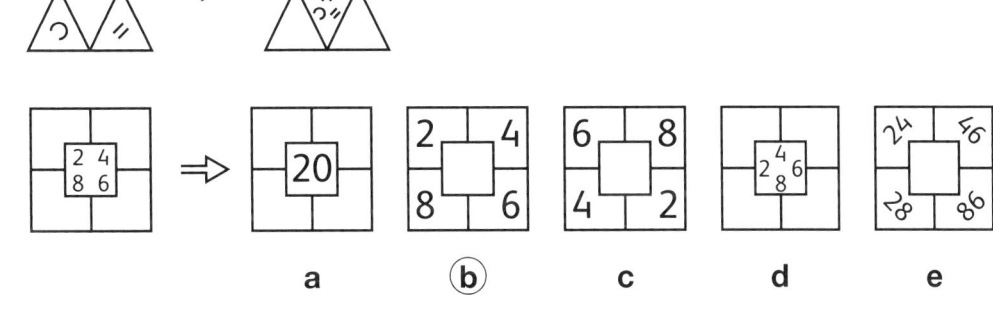

a **b** **c** **d** **e**

The answer is **b**.

Now try these. Match the missing part of the second pair in a similar way to the first pair. Circle the letter under the missing part.

1.

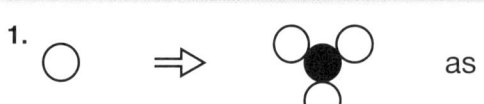

as

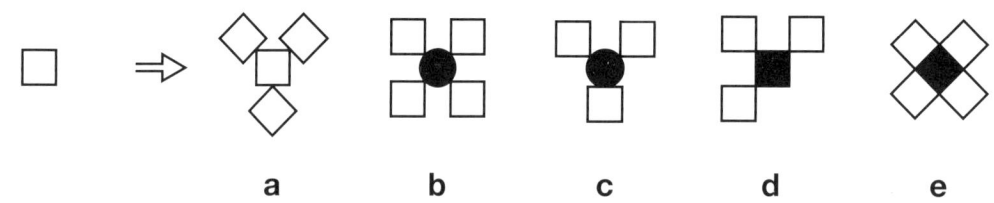

    a   b   c   d   e

2.

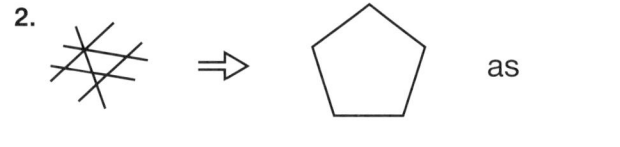

as

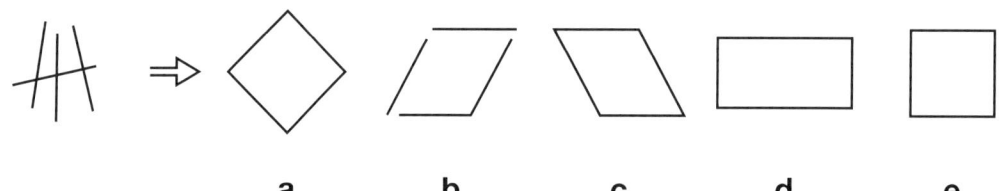

    a   b   c   d   e

3.

as

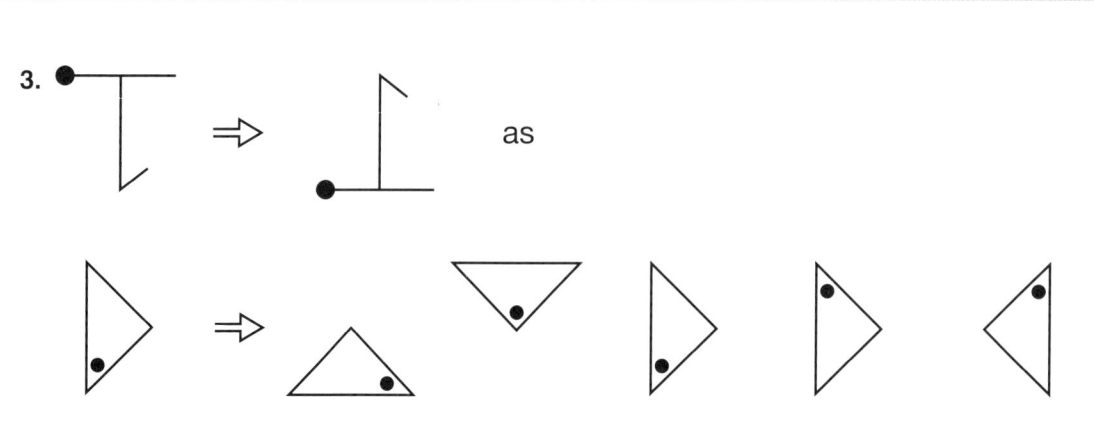

    a   b   c   d   e

4.

            a   b   c   d   e

5.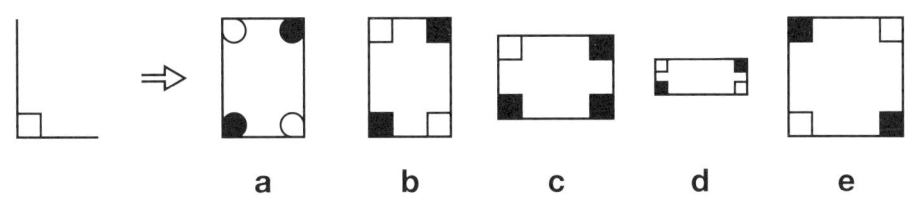

            a   b   c   d   e

6.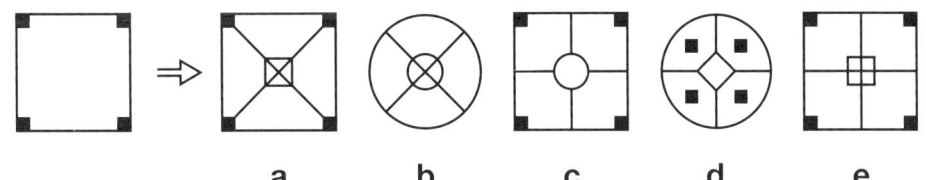

            a   b   c   d   e

7.

            a   b   c   d   e

/7

Example

Find the shape or pattern which completes the sequence.
Circle the letter under it.

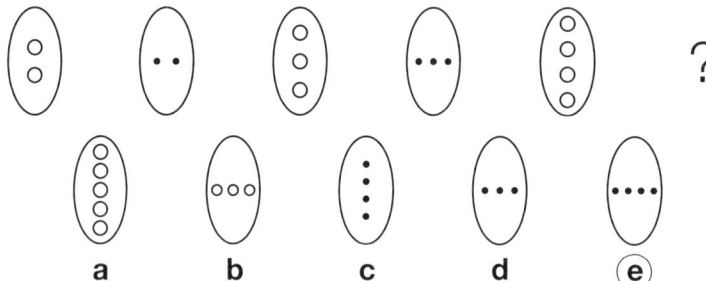

The answer is **e** because the pattern is large circles in a vertical line, followed by the same number of small black circles in a horizontal line.

Now try these. Find the shape or pattern which completes the sequence.
Circle the letter under it.

8.

| 6 ☐ 4 | 9 ◇ ㇀ | 3 ☐ 4 | ? | 9 ☐ 4 |

| 6 ◇ ㇀ | 9 ☐ 4 | 3 ◇ ㇀ | 9 ◇ 4 | 6 ☐ ㇀ |
| **a** | **b** | **c** | **d** | **e** |

9.

| | | | ? | |
| **a** | **b** | **c** | **d** | **e** |

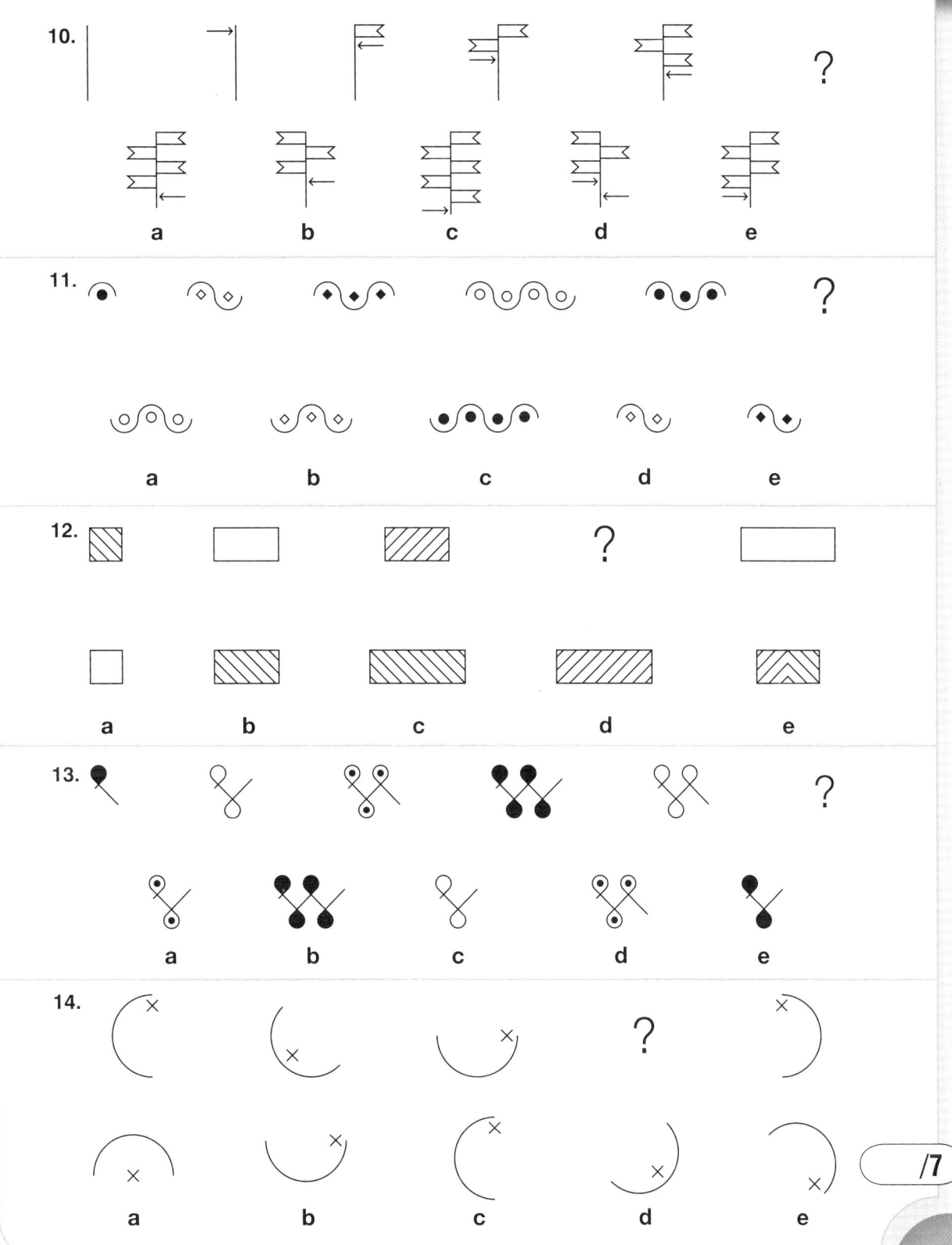

10.

a   b   c   d   e

11.

a   b   c   d   e

12.

a   b   c   d   e

13.

a   b   c   d   e

14.

a   b   c   d   e

/7

Example

Complete the grid by finding the missing square.
Circle the letter under the square.

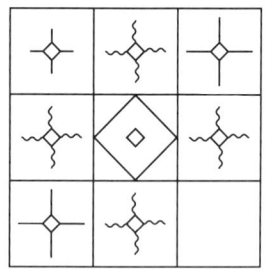

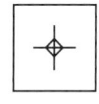   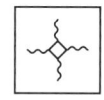   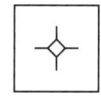   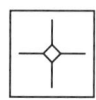

a   b   ⓒ   d   e

The answer is **c** because the outer squares of the grid are the same on the diagonal.

Now try these. Complete the grid by finding the missing square.
Circle the letter under the square.

15.

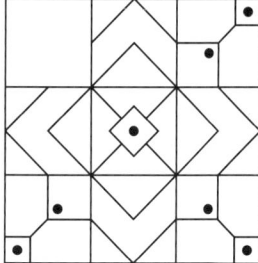

a   b   c   d   e

16.

S	2	f	2	S
f		2	S	2
2	S	2	S	f
S	f	S	2	2
2	2	S	f	S

2		f		S		S		2
a		b		c		d		e

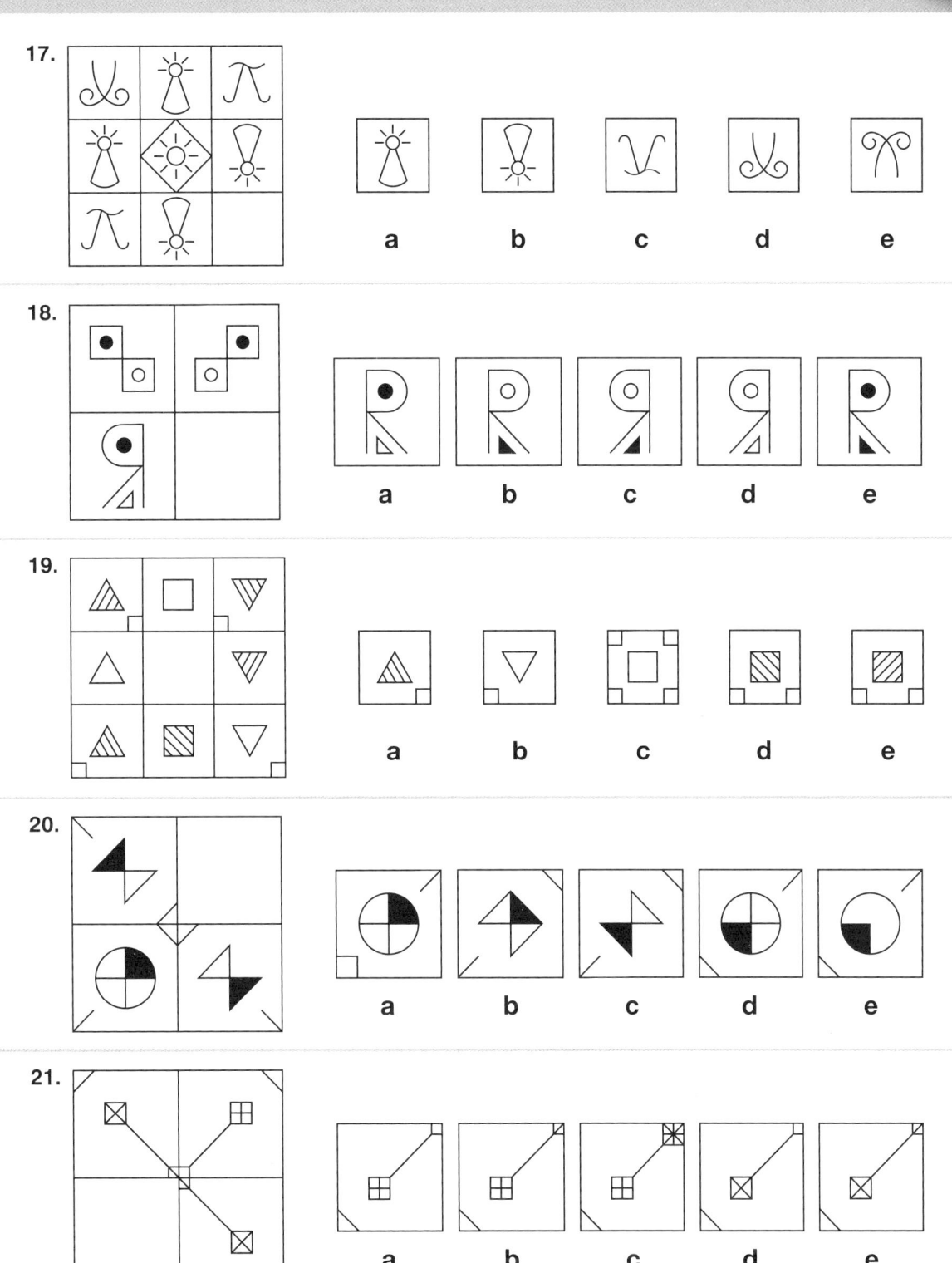

17.

a b c d e

18.

a b c d e

19.

a b c d e

20.

a b c d e

21.

a b c d e

Example

Look at the patterns and letter codes to work out the new code. Circle the letter under the code.

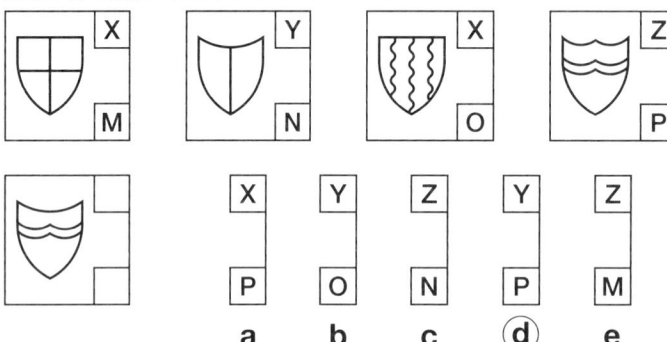

a   b   c   **d**   e

The answer is **d**. X, Y and Z are the codes for the shield shape. M, N, O and P are the codes for the patterns on the shields. In this case, the shield is Y and the pattern is P, so **d** is circled.

Now try these. Look at the patterns and letter codes to work out the new code. Circle the letter under the code.

22.

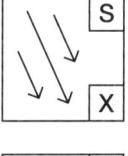
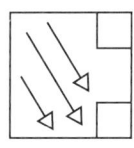
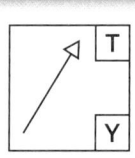
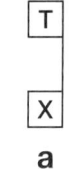

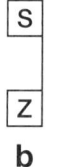
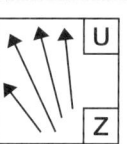
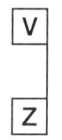

a   b   c   d   e

23.

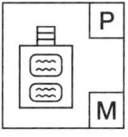
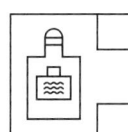
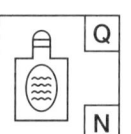
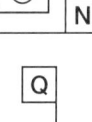
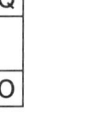
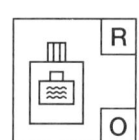
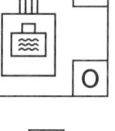

a   b   c   d   e

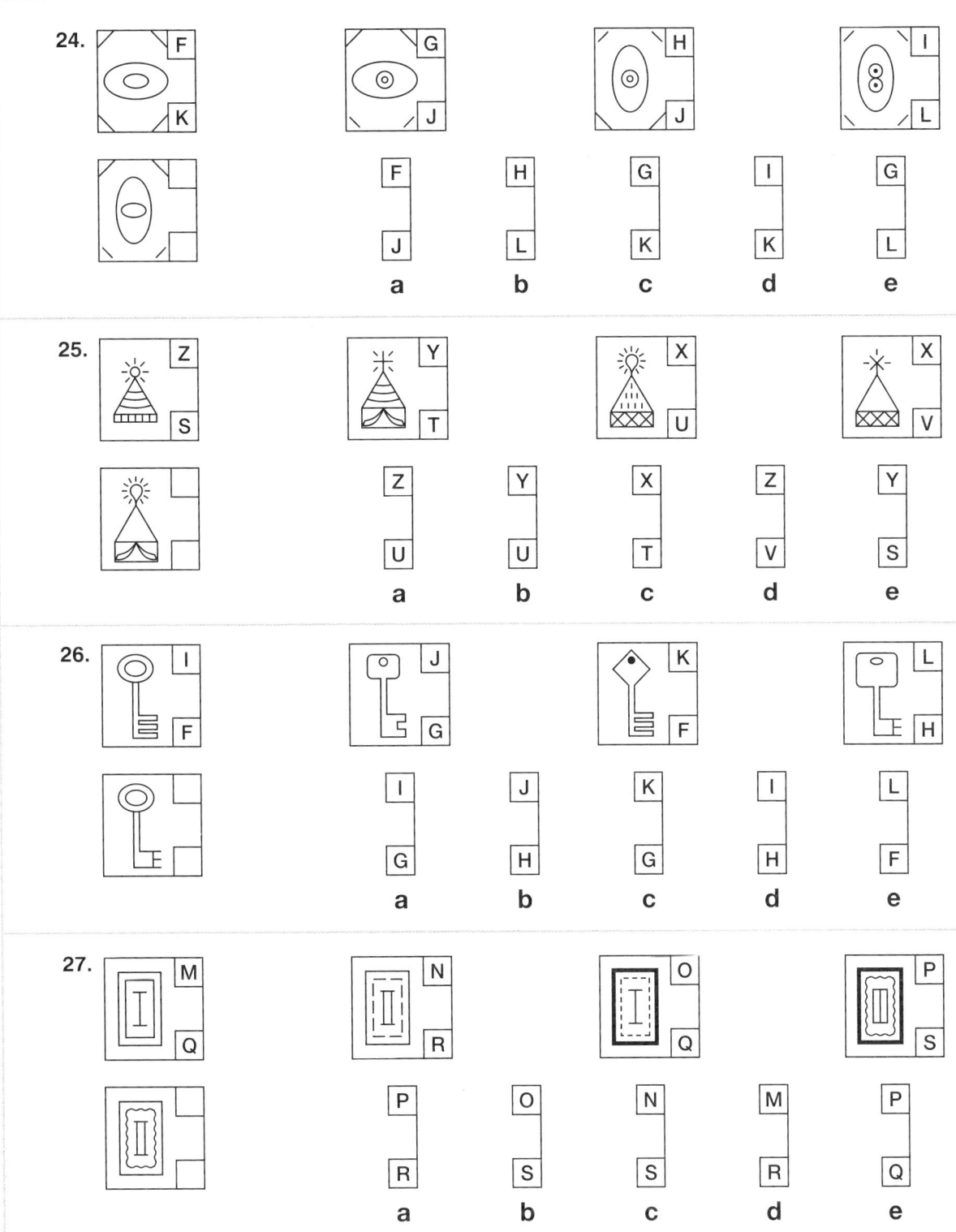

28.

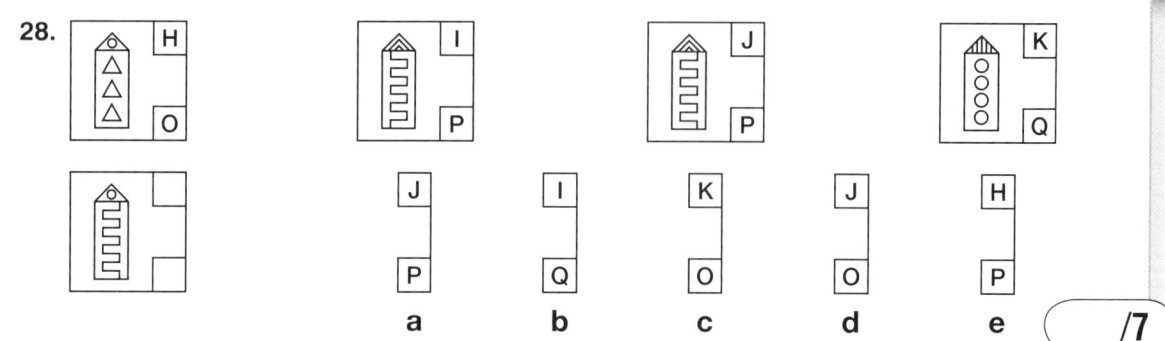

a   b   c   d   e   /7

Example

Choose the shape or pattern from the right-hand side which belongs to the set on the left-hand side. Circle the letter under it.

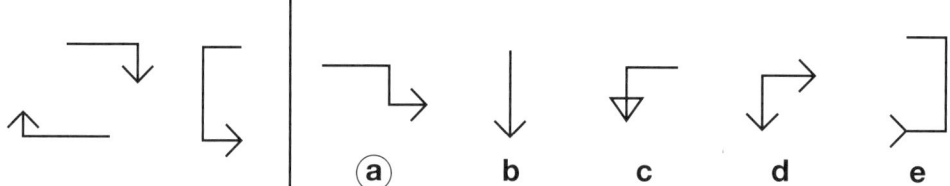

The answer is **a** as it is the only one that completes the set.

It cannot be the other shapes because **b** is a straight arrow, **c** has the wrong arrow head, **d** has two arrow heads and in **e**, the arrow is reversed.

Now try these. Choose the shape or pattern from the right-hand side which belongs to the set on the left-hand side. Circle the letter under it.

29.

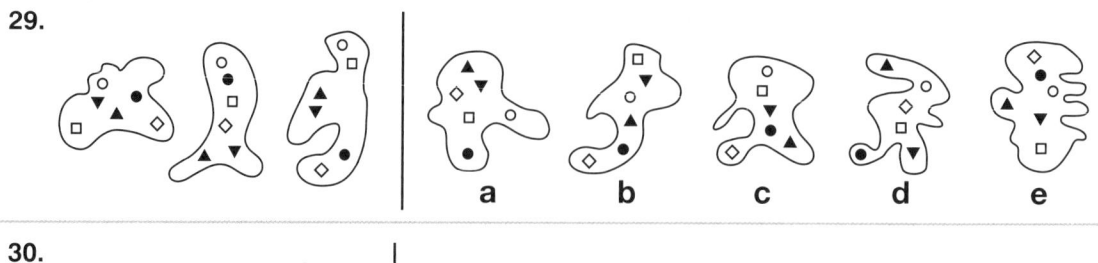

30.

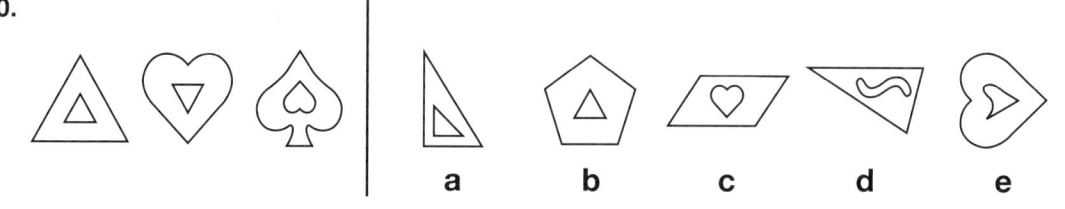

31.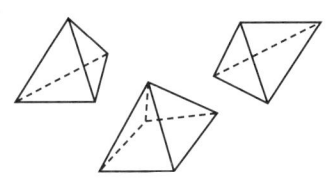

 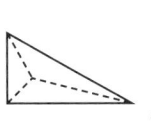 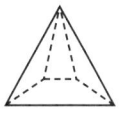 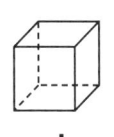 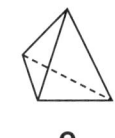

   a   **b**   **c**   **d**   **e**

32.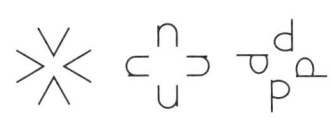

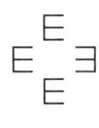   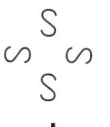

   a   **b**   **c**   **d**   **e**

33.

   a   **b**   **c**   **d**   **e**

34.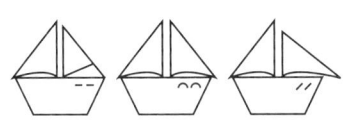

 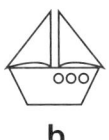   

   a   **b**   **c**   **d**   **e**

35.

   a   **b**   **c**   **d**   **e**

/7

/35

PAPER 6

Example

Find the shape or pattern which completes the sequence.
Circle the letter under it.

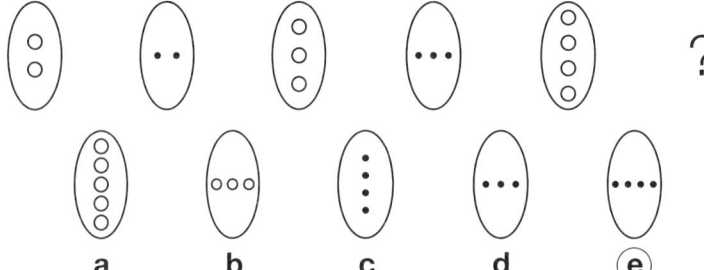

The answer is **e** because the pattern is large circles in a vertical line, followed by the same number of small black circles in a horizontal line.

Now try these. Find the shape or pattern which completes the sequence.
Circle the letter under it.

1.

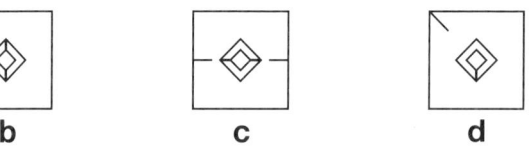

2.

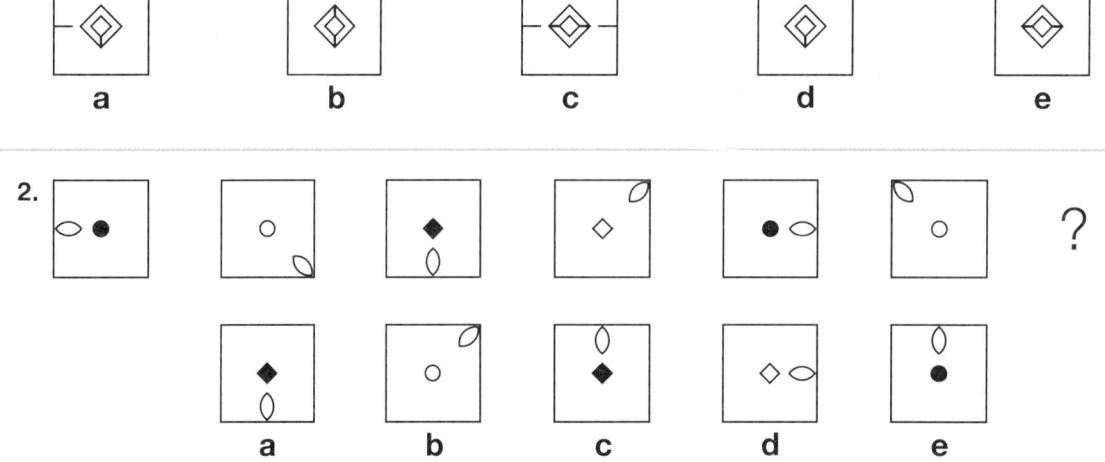

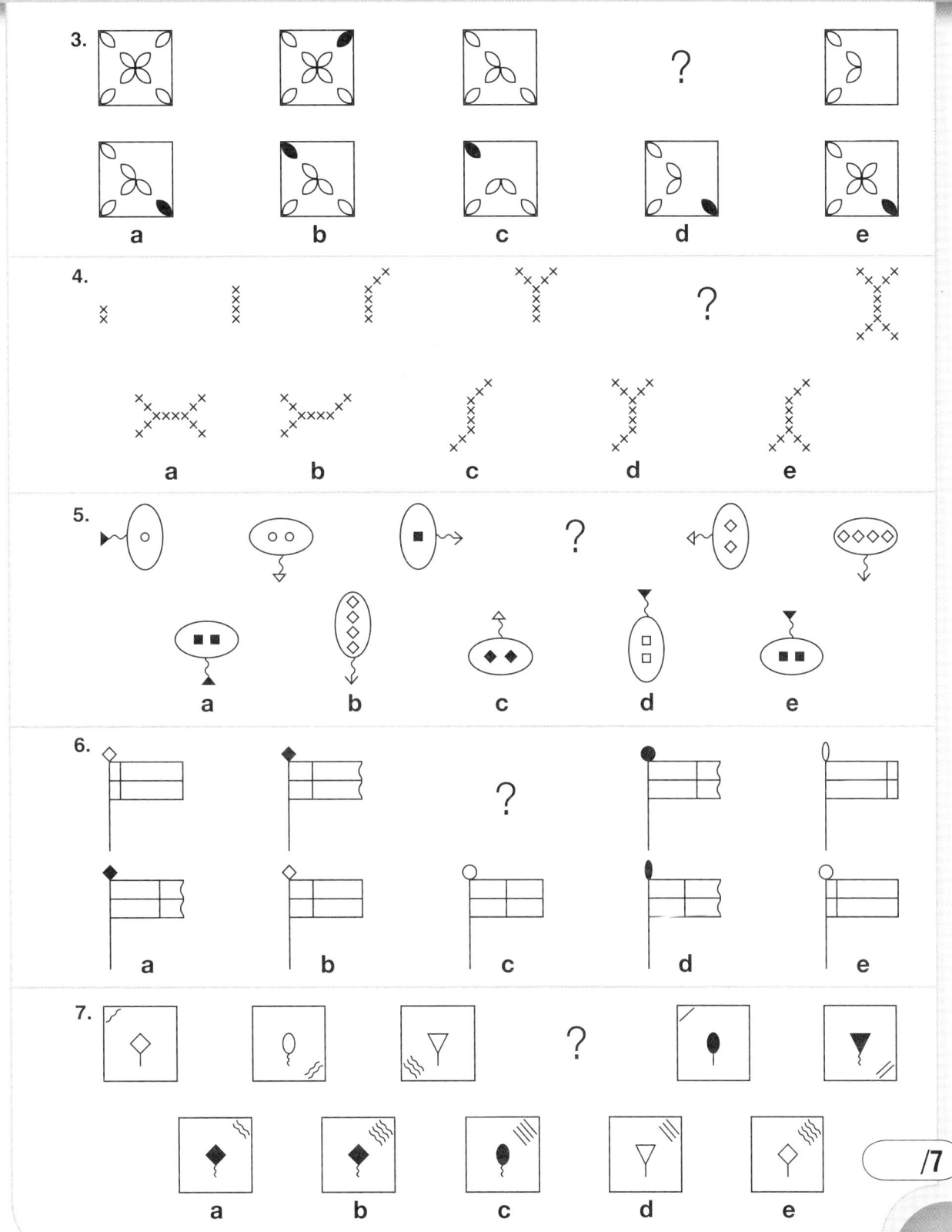

Example

Choose the shape or pattern from the right-hand side which belongs to the set on the left-hand side. Circle the letter under it.

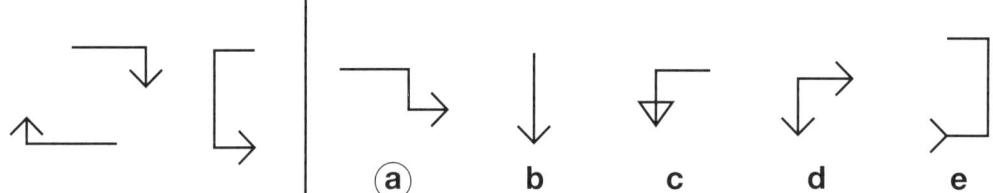

| | a | b | c | d | e |

The answer is **a** as it is the only one that completes the set.

It cannot be the other shapes because **b** is a straight arrow, **c** has the wrong arrow head, **d** has two arrow heads and in **e**, the arrow is reversed.

Now try these. Choose the shape or pattern from the right-hand side which belongs to the set on the left-hand side. Circle the letter under it.

8.

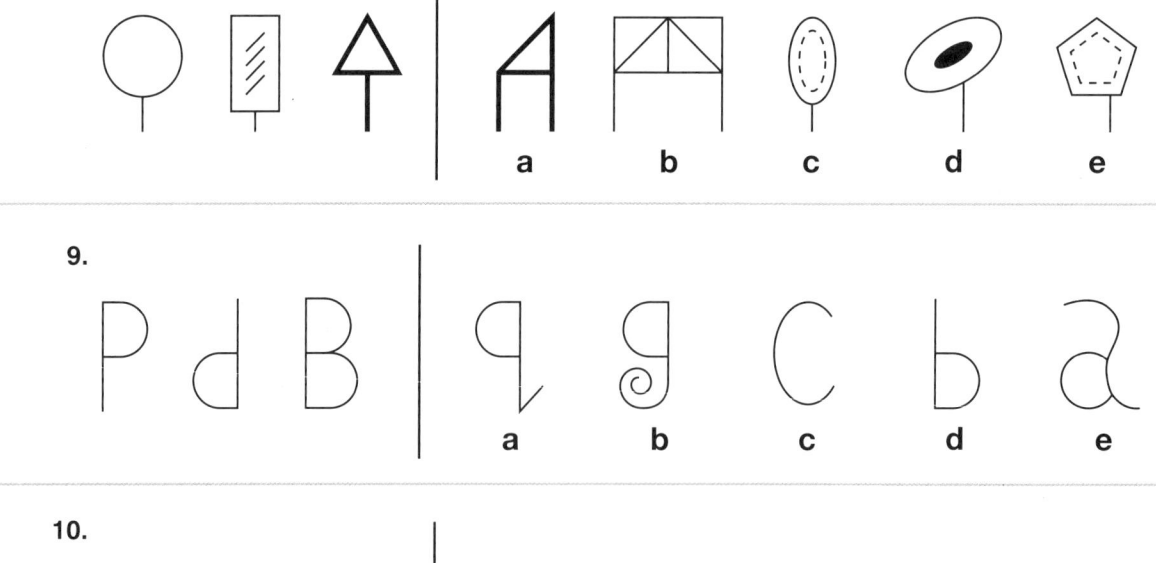

9.

10.

11.

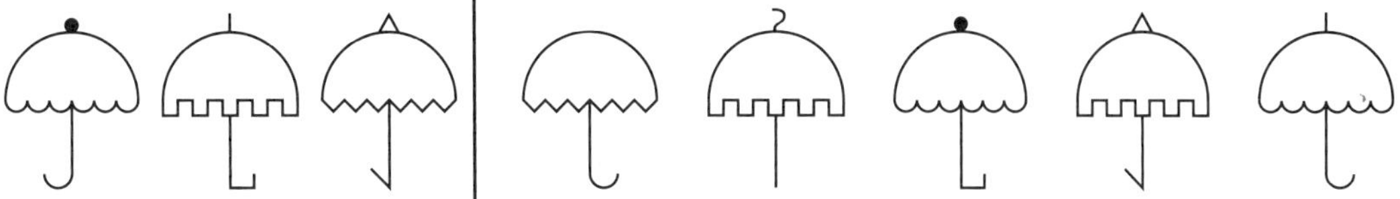

a b c d e

12.

a b c d e

13.

a b c d e

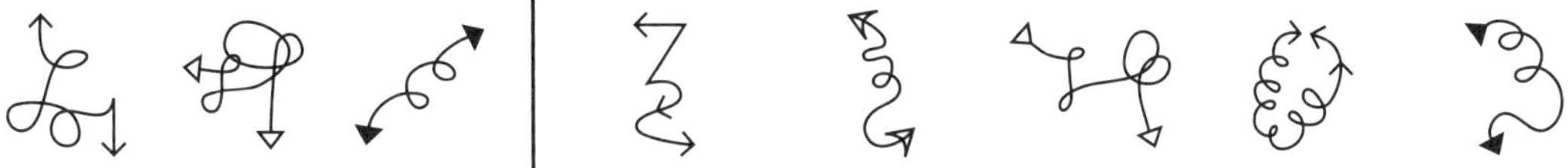

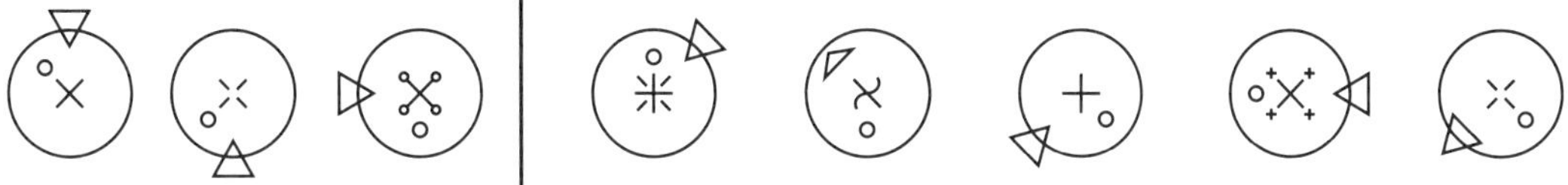

14.

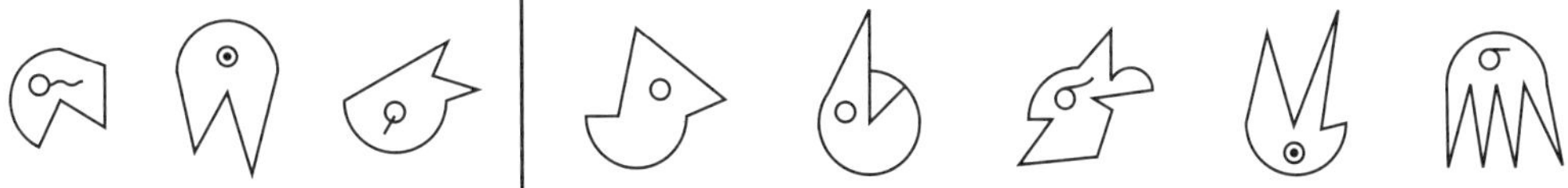

a b c d e

/7

Example

Match the missing part of the second pair in a similar way to the first pair. Circle the letter under the missing part.

as

a (b) c d e

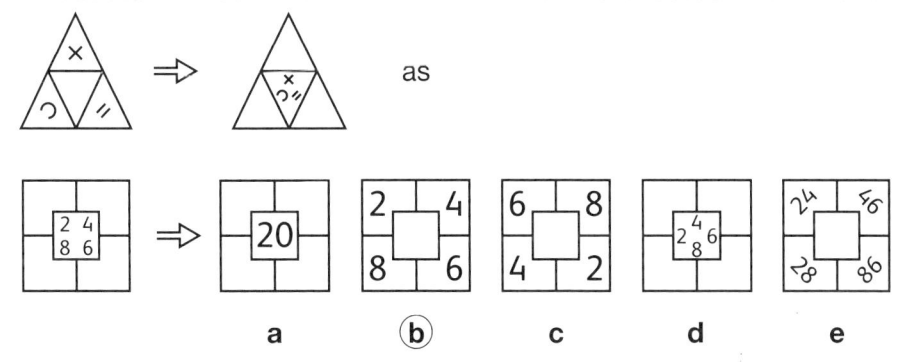

The answer is **b**.

Now try these. Match the missing part of the second pair in a similar way to the first pair. Circle the letter under the missing part.

15. ⇒   as

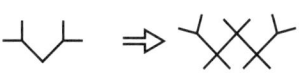 ⇒ 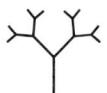   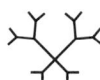   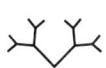   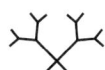

    a   **b**   **c**   **d**   **e**

16. 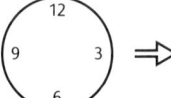 ⇒   as

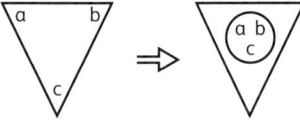 ⇒    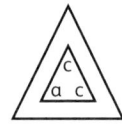      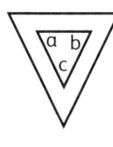

    a   **b**   **c**   **d**   **e**

17. 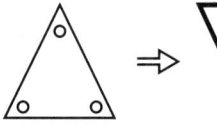   as

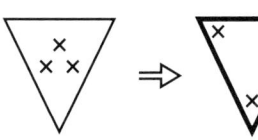          

    a   **b**   **c**   **d**   **e**

18. 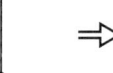   as

    a   **b**   **c**   **d**   **e**

19. 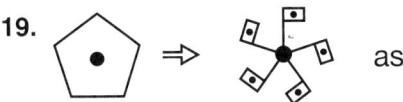 as

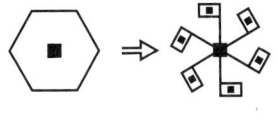

a   b   c   d   e

20. 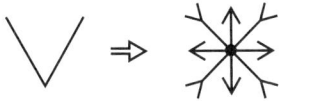 as

  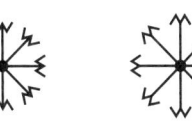

a   b   c   d   e

21.  as

a   b   c   d   e

/7

Example

Complete the grid by finding the missing square.
Circle the letter under the square.

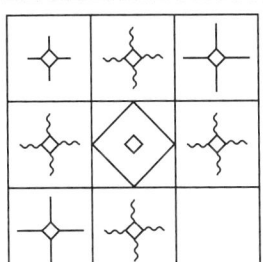

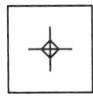 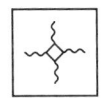 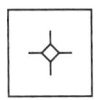 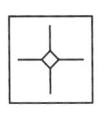 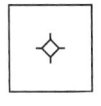

a   b   ⓒ   d   e

The answer is **c** because the outer squares of the grid are the same on the diagonal.

Now try these. Complete the grid by finding the missing square. Circle the letter under the square.

22.

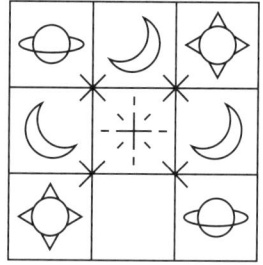         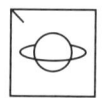

                     a   b   c   d   e

23.

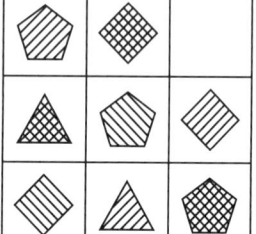

                     a   b   c   d   e

24.

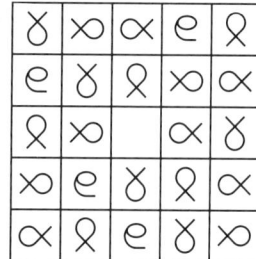

                     a   b   c   d   e

25.

                     a   b   c   d   e

26.

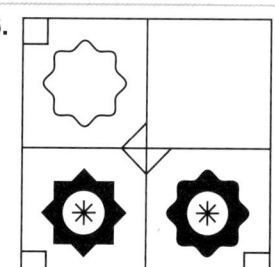   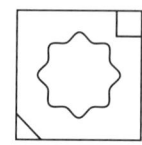   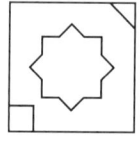   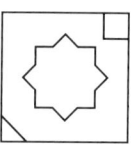   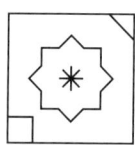   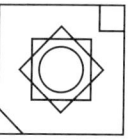

                     a   b   c   d   e

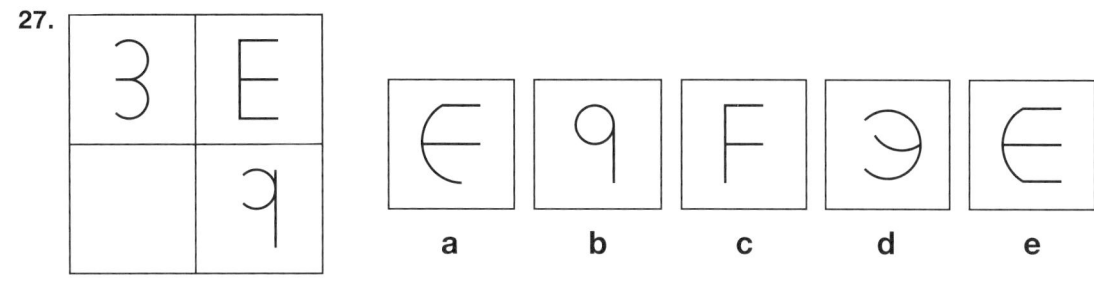

27.

a   b   c   d   e

28.

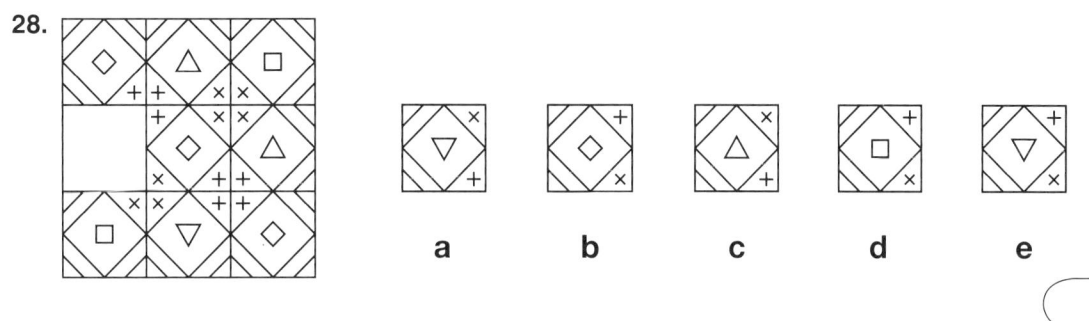

a   b   c   d   e

/7

Example

Look at the patterns and letter codes to work out the new code.
Circle the letter under the code.

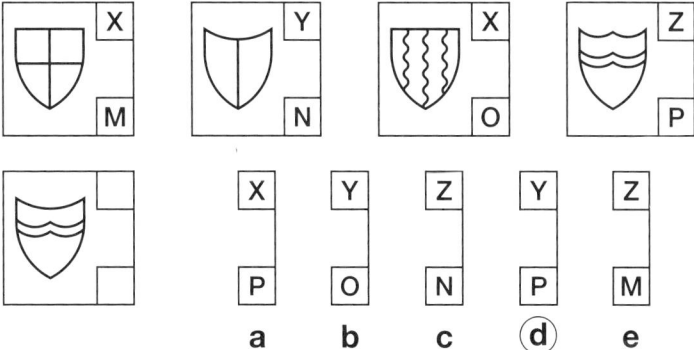

a   b   c   **d**   e

The answer is **d**. X, Y and Z are the codes for the shield shape. M, N, O and P are the codes for the patterns on the shields. In this case, the shield is Y and the pattern is P, so **d** is circled.

Now try these. Look at the patterns and letter codes to work out the new code. Circle the letter under the code.

29.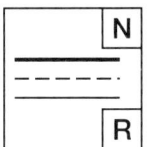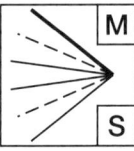

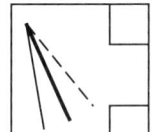

O	M	N	N	O
R	U	T	U	S
a	**b**	**c**	**d**	**e**

30.

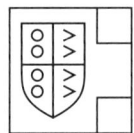

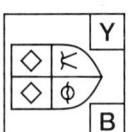 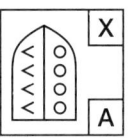

W	Y	X	X	Y
B	A	B	C	C
a	**b**	**c**	**d**	**e**

31.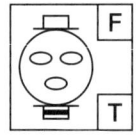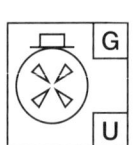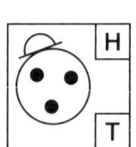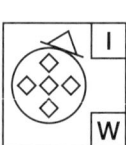

G	F	H	H	I
W	W	U	T	U
a	**b**	**c**	**d**	**e**

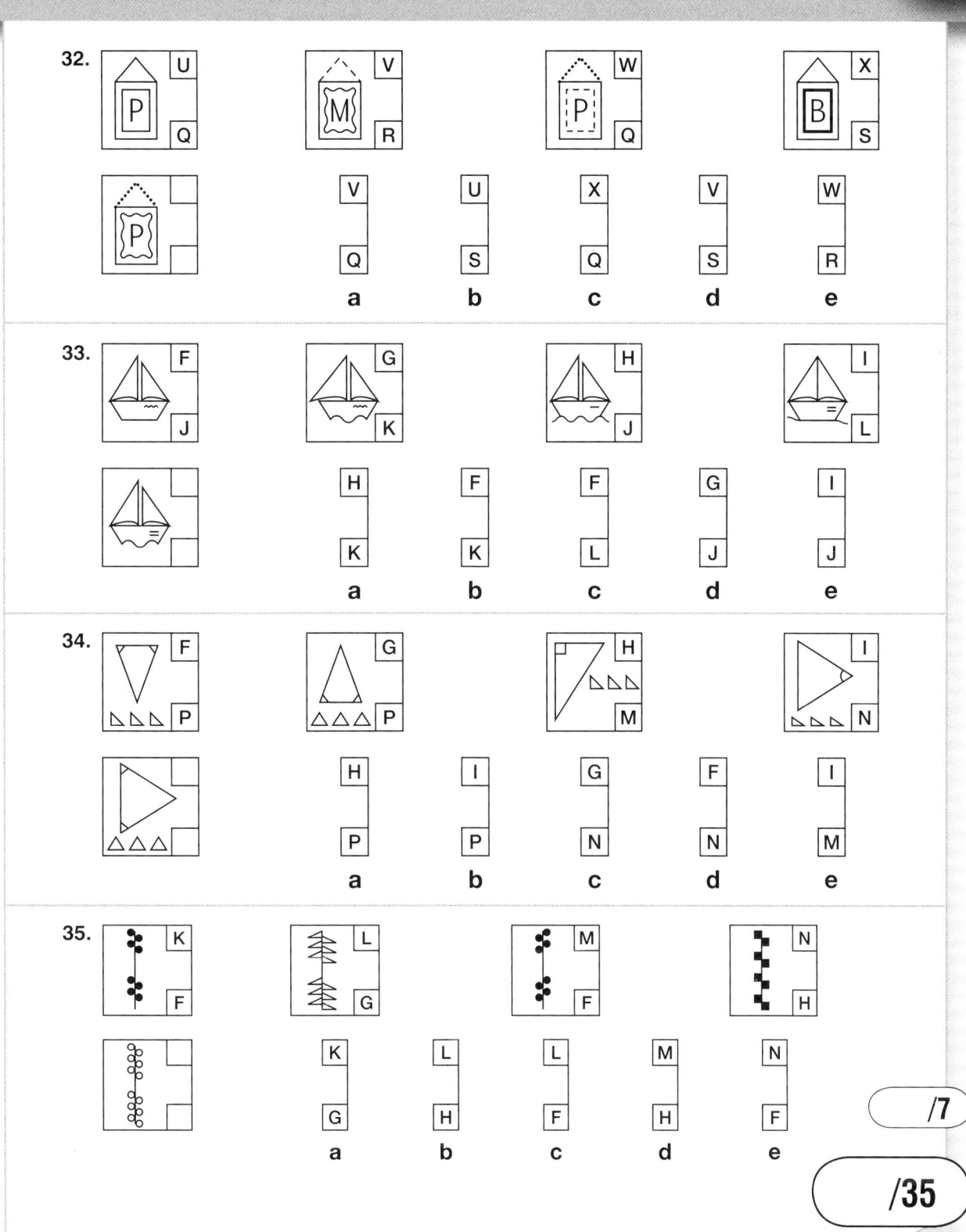

32.

a   b   c   d   e

33.

a   b   c   d   e

34.

a   b   c   d   e

35.

a   b   c   d   e

/7

/35

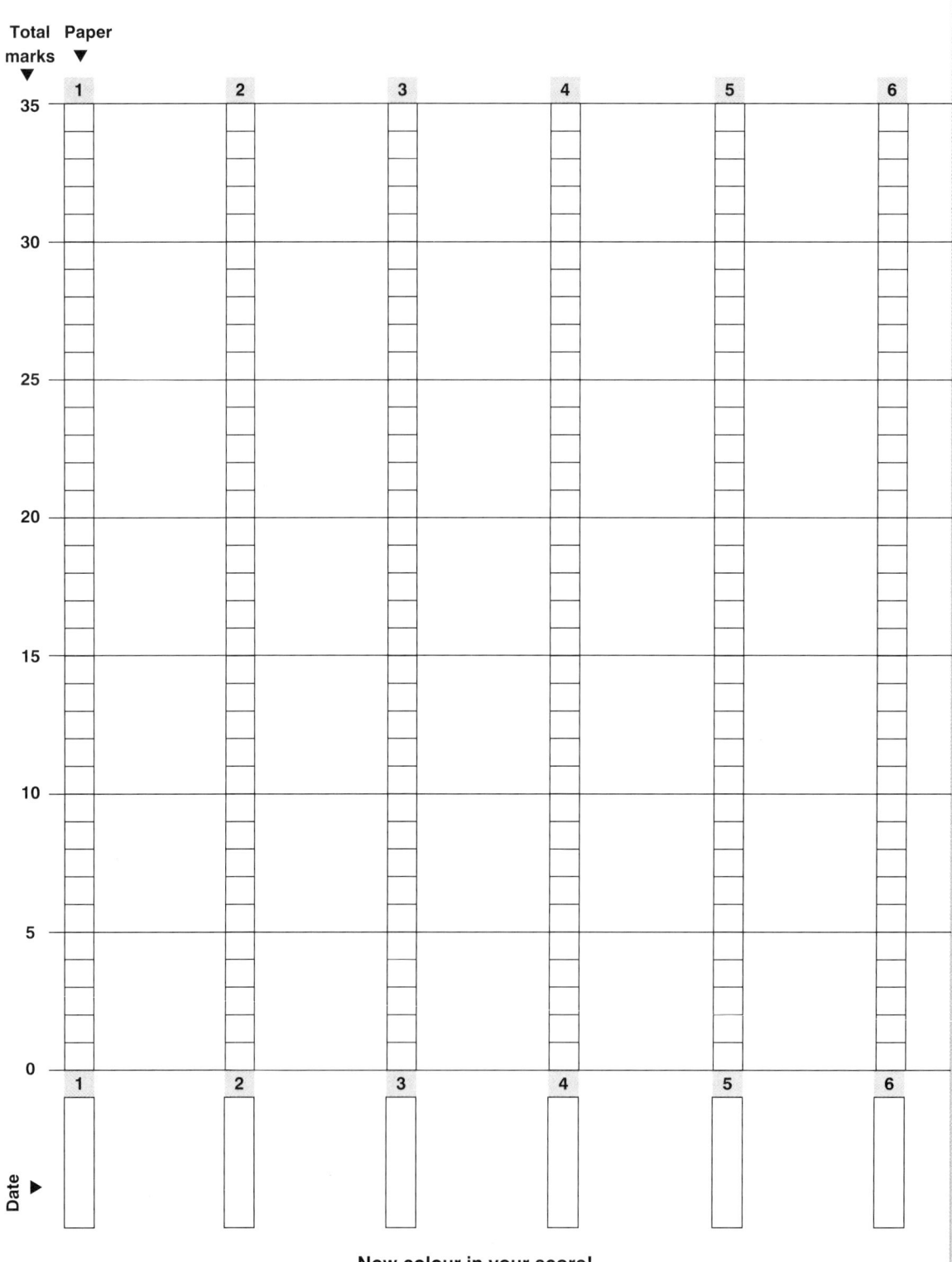

Total **Paper**
marks ▼

Date ▶

Now colour in your score!